SPEECH SCIENCE

Acoustics in Speech

SPEECH SCIENCE

ACOUSTICS IN SPEECH

(Second Edition, Fourth Printing)

By

RICHARD A. HOOPS, Ph.D.

Director, Speech and Hearing Clinic
Ball State University
Muncie, Indiana

CHARLES C THOMAS • PUBLISHER
Springfield • Illinois • U.S.A.

Published and Distributed throughout the World by
CHARLES C THOMAS • PUBLISHER
BANNERSTONE HOUSE
301-327 East Lawrence Avenue, Springfield, Illinois, U.S.A.

© *1960 and 1969, by* CHARLES C THOMAS • PUBLISHER
ISBN 0-398-00869-8
Library of Congress Catalog Card Number: 69-12058

First Edition, 1960
Second Edition, First Printing, 1969
Second Edition, Second Printing, 1972
Second Edition, Third Printing, 1973
Second Edition, Fourth Printing, 1976

*With THOMAS BOOKS careful attention is given to all details of
manufacturing and design. It is the Publisher's desire to present books
that are satisfactory as to their physical qualities and artistic possibilities
and appropriate for their particular use. THOMAS BOOKS will be true
to those laws of quality that assure a good name and good will.*

Printed in the United States of America
00-2

TO
BO

PREFACE

O NE OF THE GREATEST AREAS of difficulty for most students beginning the Speech Pathology and Audiology sequence is the field of acoustics. Perhaps one reason for the difficulty in reacting to the science of sound is simply the fact that one cannot touch it, one cannot smell it, one cannot see it. We are talking about a phenomenon which is present, and ask students to accept our word for the fact that it is present, and depend upon our word for their evidence. If one could see sound wave movements, one would be in a much better position to understand the actual nature of the transmission of sound. In the first chapter some examples will be given of laboratory experiments which may be of help in obtaining a visual impression of sound waves. For the moment, however, the student is asked to accept, on face value, the fact that sound does occur and that its behavior can be described.

RICHARD A. HOOPS, PH.D.

INTRODUCTION

THE AREA OF SPEECH and hearing therapy has come a far distance from its beginning in the 1920's. Today there are some thirteen thousand members of the American Speech and Hearing Association, and an even greater number of practicing speech and hearing therapists in the public schools of the nation.

These individuals come from widely divergent educational backgrounds as they enroll in college or university programs in Speech Pathology and Audiology. Therefore they are challenged to differing degrees by the course work in the physics of sound and voice production which usually forms a portion of this training program. In many university programs, persons training for careers in acoustics or general speech are also enrolled in this type of course.

Speech and hearing therapy students at Ball State University are ordinarily not bewildered by course material dealing with specific speech or hearing impediments, but, due to limited backgrounds in the study of physics, have difficulty understanding terms such as the *bel,* the *decibel,* a *resonator,* or other concepts with which they must become familiar if they are to be adequately trained to deal with speech and hearing problems. In correspondence with instructors at other colleges and universities, the author has reached the conclusion that students in many programs share the same problem.

There is nothing particularly new about the material in this book. Most of it has been available before in various textbooks and journal articles. The attempt in the present book is twofold: (1) to put all this data into one book, and (2) to present it in a meaningful way to individuals meeting the material for the first time. In many cases, discussion has been included which demonstrates the application of some of the acoustical material in the field of Speech Pathology and Audiology. This is particularly true in the areas of hearing loss and voice problems.

The author hopes these two goals are realized in the present publication. The author will of course be grateful for any suggestions as to possible revision.

ACKNOWLEDGMENTS

THIS BOOK COULD NOT HAVE BEEN WRITTEN without the aid of the many students during the past twelve years who have dealt with the original version and pointed out the difficulties and the sections where clarity was lacking, and have responded in similar fashion during the course of revision. The same comment applies to my wife, who has also taught from the original text and urged reconsideration. I am grateful for her help, her persistence and her patience.

I should also like to express my appreciation to the many publishers who gave permission to reprint illustrations from the following sources: Acoustical Society of America, for references in the *Journal of the Acoustical Society of America;* American Speech and Hearing Association, for references in the *Journal of Speech and Hearing Research;* Appleton-Century-Crofts, Inc., for references in Judson and Weaver, *Voice Science;* Bell Telephone Laboratories, for references in Denes and Pinson, *The Speech Chain;* Doubleday and Company, Inc., for references in Van Bergeijk, Pierce, and David, *Waves and the Ear;* Harper and Brothers, for references in Fairbanks, *Voice and Articulation Drillbook;* Holt, Rinehart, and Winston, for references in Davis and Silverman, *Hearing and Deafness,* and Hanley and Thurman, *Developing Vocal Skills;* McGraw-Hill Book Company, Inc., for references in Culver, *Musical Acoustics;* D. Van Nostrand Company, Inc. for references in Fletcher, *Speech and Hearing in Communication;* and to John Wiley and Sons, Inc., for references in Stevens and Davis, *Hearing, Its Psychology and Physiology;* Boring, Langfeld, and Weld, *Foundations of Psychology;* and Stevens, *Handbook of Experimental Psychology.* These companies have been most cooperative in this endeavor.

R.A.H.

CONTENTS

PART ONE

FREQUENCY AND RESONANCE

PART TWO

TIME, INTENSITY, AND QUALITY

SPEECH SCIENCE

Acoustics in Speech

PART ONE

FREQUENCY AND RESONANCE

I

SOUND

SOUND IS A CONDITION of disturbance of the particles of an elastic medium which is propagated in a wave outward in all directions from a vibrating body, and takes the form of displacement of the particles forward and backward from their positions of rest in the direction of the propagation of the wave (1).

The basic concept involved in this definition is that a sound wave is composed of what actually is happening to a number of individual molecules of air, or any other medium, when they are involved with a vibratory action. In spite of the fact that sound is invisible and intangible, one can still define the elements necessary for its existence, and these are four in nature. These four elements are the following:

1. A source of energy: There must always be a force applied to a vibrator to make it vibrate. In the human voice, the force against the vocal folds is air coming from the lungs. In a reed instrument (e.g., clarinet, oboe), this same energy is applied to a vibrating reed. In a brass instrument (e.g., trumpet, trombone), this energy is applied to the vibrating lips of the musician. In a piano, the fingers of the pianist apply energy to the keys, which in turn force hammers to strike strings within the piano.

2. The vibrator: The vibrator is an object which undergoes molecular activity in such a fashion that the molecules of the object are disturbed from positions of rest and move in a to and fro movement. Practically all inanimate objects may serve as vibrators if they are struck. The strings of a stringed instrument, or the reed of a reed instrument, or the lips of a trumpet player, or the tines of a tuning fork, all may serve as vibrators.

5

3. A transmitting medium: In order for sound to move it must move through some substance which is composed of molecules. Ordinarily the medium in which we are accustomed to finding sound is air. Other media through which sound can travel are water, or any other liquid; or any solid object. The medium must be elastic, containing particles capable of returning to a position of rest after disturbance. It must also consist of a mass which may be any source capable of vibratory motion. The point of this discussion is to indicate that in the absence of matter sound cannot be conducted. For example, sound does not travel through a vacuum, and therefore sound does not travel through interplanetary space in which there is no atmosphere. It must be understood that the medium in which sound is propagated is always a three dimensional medium, and the sound is transmitted in that medium in all directions.

4. A receiving mechanism: The human receiving mechanism transforms acoustical energy into mechanical, hydraulic and then electrochemical energy. The end result of this process is the psychological response known as hearing. From the purely physical standpoint this element is not requisite to the existence of sound; from the viewpoint of the psychologist, however, it is.

Let us turn our attention in greater detail to the concept of vibration. This has already been defined as movement to and fro. A medium exists, is complacent, and then is suddenly disturbed. Something has upset the normal state of things at some point in the medium and the disturbance thus created expands, spherically. Almost any object we can name, if struck sharply, or moved rapidly through air, can serve as a vibrator. There are, however, two main classes of vibration which should be listed. The first of these is a periodic type of vibration, one in which the vibration repeats itself in a regular pattern, and in equal intervals of time. Such a periodic vibrator produces a type of motion called either periodic or harmonic motion. Periodic sound is tonal in character. Its waves are regular and can be defined with respect to dimension and composition. Vibrating reeds or strings of musical instruments, organ pipes and human vocal folds are among the vibrators producing periodic sounds.

Sounds produced by periodic vibration can be classified as musical tones. Pure tones, tones in which there is only one frequency component, are produced by simple periodic or harmonic motion of a vibrator. Complex tones, on the other hand, are produced by *complex* periodic motion of a vibrator: "Any complex periodic motion can be analyzed into a series of simple harmonic components . . . given any periodic motion having a fundamental frequency 'n,' the same motion can be reduced to one particular set of simple harmonic motions of suitable amplitudes and phases whose frequencies are n, 2n, 3n, 4n, etc." (2).

Opposed to periodic vibration is that form known as aperiodic vibration. This is vibration in an erratic or nonregular pattern. Sounds produced by such vibrations are classified as noises. Such sounds do not repeat themselves in a rhythmic pattern. They consist of vibrators producing acoustic events which happened once and are not repeated in a standard fashion. We describe such sounds as noise, thumps, hisses, scratches, or some other verbiage intended to describe something which is not particularly pleasing.

Regardless of the type of vibrator serving as a source of sound, however, some factors are found in common. The vibrator introduces change into the sound medium, either regularly (periodically) or irregularly (aperiodically) upsetting and regrouping spatial relationships among particles of air or some other medium.

Conditions requisite to the occurrence of vibration are elasticity, inertia and a small damping factor. The vibrator must be composed of an "elastic" substance; the particles within it must be capable of displacement and rebound. Elasticity, then, is simply the tendency of a medium to resume its original or normal condition after some change has been introduced.

Inertia has been defined as the tendency of a body at rest to remain at rest, or a body in motion to remain in motion. Inertia then is the tendency for an object or medium or a particle to keep on doing what it has been doing without changing. So inertia and elasticity can be thought of as being antagonists in the transmission of sound. If the particle is at rest, inertia wishes to keep it that way. However, when vibrated, elasticity permits movement. Once the body is moving inertia wants to keep it moving, but elasticity steps in to say "No, you must stop going this way and go back from whence you came."

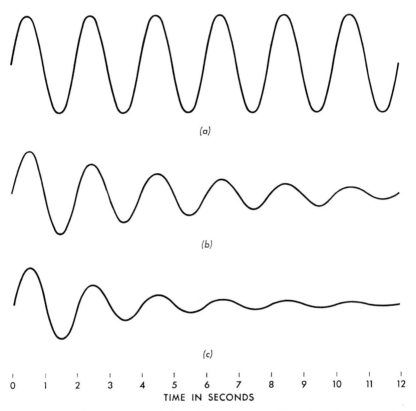

FIGURE 1. Displacements of the vibrating mass with and without damping: (a) no loss; (b) lightly damped; (c) more heavily damped. (Reprinted with permission from Denes and Pinson, *The Speech Chain,* 1963, Bell Telephone Laboratories.)

The damping factor is simply an interfering force in the production of sound, or anything that works to block vibration. We have good illustrations of damping factors in operation when we are trying to soundproof a room. Usually we require acoustic tile on the ceiling and sometimes on the walls of a room if we want to reduce the amount of vibratory action from the molecules of air contained within that room. These acoustic tile panels set up traps for molecules, thus effectively reducing the amount of vibration which can be carried by the molecules in the room. More along this line of thought will be discussed during the section on resonance and reflection of sounds.

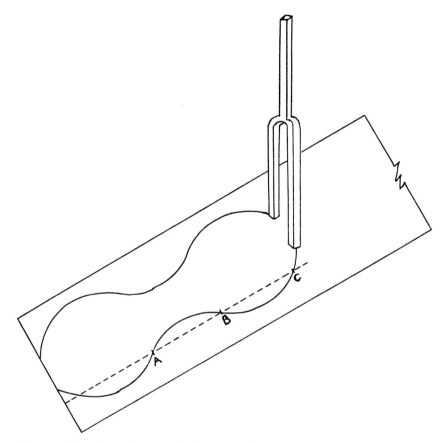

FIGURE 2. The production of sine waves by a tuning fork. Points A, B and C represent the points in the cycle when the vibrator is passing through its position of rest. AC represents one complete cycle.

We can actually see some examples of sound if we were to have the proper equipment for laboratory experimentation. For example, if a strip of emulsified paper is drawn past a vibrating tuning fork so that the fork is just perpendicular to the paper and just barely touching it, the emulsion removed by the tips of the prongs of the tuning fork will trace sinusoidal curves on the paper. These sinusoidal curves would represent the vibratory characteristics of the molecules in the prongs of the tuning fork. If the prongs put too much pressure against the paper, a damping factor is created and the vibration will cease.

Probably the best method of obtaining a better idea of the vibratory characteristics of sound would be to look at sound traveling through a solid object placed upon the plastic film of the grid in an electron microscope. With such equipment and with a correct light source to give visual images of the molecular activity within the box, the actual molecules of the solid could be seen moving to and fro as the sound impinges upon the object. The sound used would have to be of extremely high frequency (so high that the human ear could not detect it) and carefully chosen in an attempt to create standing waves. The usual illustration of sound used in a physics class utilizes standing waves (a sound wave which makes no progress through a tube, but instead keeps repeating itself over and over). A tube is dusted evenly on the inside with powder, the sound is directed into one end, and disturbances can be seen in the powder. One will discover that the powder forms into pockets, and that the pockets are separated by sections of the tube containing no powder.

A more homely and perhaps more practical demonstration of vibration is to simply throw a rock into a pool of water. When the stone hits the pond, ripples spread outward in ever expanding perfect circles. Now, in this case, the ripples are not being created by the sound of the rock hitting the water but rather by the impact upon the surface of the water by a foreign body striking it, and whereas the illustration is not a perfect one, it is analogous to the way that sound waves behave.

The chief reason for the lack of perfection in the preceding example is the fact that particles or molecules of water, when disturbed by a foreign body hitting the surface of the water, do not behave in the same fashion as molecules of air or some other medium when disturbed by a sound. Returning to the example of the stone hitting the water, when the stone hits the water the impact is spread outward in a circular fashion. Each molecule of water, however, moves only up and down from its position of rest.

This can be proven by throwing out a fishing line with a bobber into the pond before throwing the stone. When the stone hits the water, the ripples spread outward, but the bobber moves only up and down as the water wave passes its position. A wave of this nature is called a horizontal wave, and is characterized by the fact that the movement of each particle is at right angles to the movement of the waves as an entire pattern. In this example, then, the movement of each molecule of water is up and down, but the movement of the wave created by the foreign object hitting the water is in an outward direction. In sound however, the movement of the molecules is along the same line of direction as the movement of the total wave. A wave of this nature is termed a longitudinal wave. Each molecule of air, or some other medium, moves backward and forward along the same direction as the outward movement of the wave.

There are three other characteristics of sound which should be discussed. The first of these is that known as frequency. Frequency is the number of complete vibrations made by a vibrator in a given unit of time; it is usually expressed in cycles per second, or in scientific publications, as Hertz. A cycle of vibration is the movement of a vibrator (or a particle thereof) from its position of rest to its maximum displacement in first one and then the opposite direction, and back again to its position of rest. In other words, when a molecule is disturbed it moves; it moves as far as it can in one direction, is returned by the elasticity of the medium, in the opposite direction, is carried by inertia past the point at which it started, and elasticity forces it to change direction once more and return in the opposite direction. The amount of movement in one direction or another of the molecule of air or other medium is determined by the amount of elasticity contained in that medium, and the force of inertia operating upon the molecules. We can also describe the frequency of vibration in terms of the time elapsing in a vibration. The time necessary for the completion of one complete cycle of vibration is termed the period. For example, if a vibrator is vibrating at 1000 times per second, which would then be called a vibration of 1000 cycles per second or Hertz, the amount of time involved for each cycle of vibration would be 1/1000 of a second. The period of this particular vibration then is 1/1000 of a second, or expressed decimally, .001 seconds. All vibrators have what is termed a "natural period." The "natural period" of the vibrator is the period (or frequency) at which the vibrating body moves most easily. Such a vibrator will vibrate for a longer period of time at that particular frequency than at any other frequency.

Frequency is a measurable characteristic of sound. One can measure frequency of vibration in a number of ways. Perhaps the easiest is to take an instrument, such as a sound oscillator, capable of producing many different frequencies and match, either by the ear or by another instrument known as an oscilloscope, some other sound which one wishes to identify with a sound produced by the sound oscillator. There is another term which should be introduced while the discussion of frequency continues, and that term is pitch. Many persons use the words frequency and pitch interchangeably. However, actually there is a difference between the two. Frequency has to do with the measurable aspect of vibration of a vibrator. It is therefore a physical phenomenon. We can, for example, measure the frequency of vibration of a telephone bell, or a pure tone in an audiometer, or a tone produced from human vocal folds. As soon as we turn to the vocal folds for our example, however, we run into conflict with the term pitch. Many persons refer to an individual's voice as being high-pitched or low-pitched. Actually pitch is not identical to frequency. Pitch has to do with the psychological interpretation of frequency. When we speak of someone's voice as being high-pitched or low-pitched, we are actually referring to the way that voice sounds to a listener. In other words, we interpret the voice as being high-pitched or low-pitched. There have been several attempts to try to quantify the concept of pitch. This research was initially carried out by persons in the field of experimental psychology. Stevens, Volkmann and Newmann (3), who were among the first to establish a relationship between pitch and frequency, devised a scale known as the Mel Scale. This scale is based on experiments in which observers, or subjects, listen to pairs of tones and report in fractions or multiples how high or low one tone sounds compared to the other. Interestingly enough, most normal listeners will show amazing similarity in their reports about these relationships between different frequencies. The experimenters arbitrarily assigned the number 1000 as the number of mels for the pitch representation of a 1000 cycle tone. They then asked the listeners to identify a tone that sounded just half as high as the tone which had been identified as 1000 mels. When the listeners agreed upon a tone as sounding half as high as the former, this latter tone was then identified as having a pitch of 500 mels. When the listeners responded by saying that another tone was simply half as high as the one which had previously been identified as having a pitch of 500 mels, this new tone was given a value of 250 mels. Pursuing in this fashion, a chart was established such as that shown in Figure 3. In the Mel Scale then, the relations between units are such that 2000 mels sounds twice as high as 1000 mels, 4000 mels sounds twice as high as 2000 mels and so forth. As is evident in the graph presented in Figure 3, the actual measurable frequency of vibration and its judged pitch relationship agree quite well up to about 2000 cycles per second. After this point, a greater change in frequency is needed to produce any change in pitch. Pitch perceptions at the higher frequencies lag behind frequency changes. A greater difference in frequency is needed at higher frequencies to establish a pitch change. The Mel Scale was developed for pure tones and has been found wanting when applied to analysis of speech. The primary reason for the inadequacy of the Mel Scale is the fact that it simply cannot cope with the many different frequencies contained in the complex tones of speech.

Another attempt at giving some kind of numerical value to the judged relationships of pitch has been to utilize a scale such as the "Equally Tempered Musical" scale. This is a system, which, although the name may be somewhat strange or foreign, is widely known. Units along the ETM Scale are octaves, tones and semi-tones. Each of these is a perceptible unit and there is no concern whether a major difference of pitch is also a perceived difference in pitch. One problem with such a scale is that as you move from one octave to another, the tones and semi-tones, although maintaining equal perceptual differences from one another, differ considerably in the actual number of cycles per second contained in the jumps. In other words the ETM scale is a sort of logarithmic scale. At low frequencies a semi-tone may consist of a very few

Speech Science

cycles per second, whereas at high frequencies a step from one semi-tone to another may consist of a fairly wide frequency jump.

The second major consideration of sound to be discussed is termed amplitude. Amplitude has to do with the amount of dis-

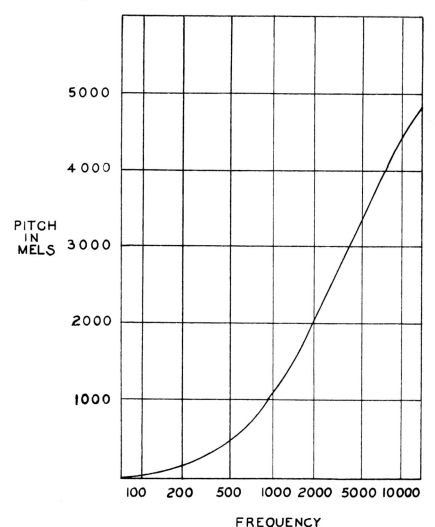

FIGURE   3. The relationship of pitch and frequency. This is a nonlinear relationship. (Reprinted with permission from Stevens and Davis, *Hearing, Its Psychology and Physiology,* 1938, John Wiley & Sons, Inc.)

tance a molecule has moved from its position of rest, first in one direction and then the other. It is readily apparent that the harder a vibrator is struck, the greater the movement will be of the molecules in that vibrator, and likewise the greater the amount of vibration in the air molecules adjacent to the vibrator. It will also be apparent that amplitude therefore will have something to do with what we in the past have called loudness. This is certainly the case; in actuality the perceptual or psychological aspect of sound which we term loudness is almost completely dependent upon the amplitude of vibration of the molecules. In this preceding sentence, we have pointed out that what we call loudness is actually a perceptual attribute of sound. It is therefore a word analogous to the word pitch. If the term loudness is analogous to the term pitch, then there must be some kind of word which has something to do with the amplitude of vibration which will be analogous to frequency. We remember that frequency is the measurable aspect, the number of times a molecule actually moves back and forth within one second.

The word connected with amplitude which is the measurable aspect of the extent of movement of the vibrator is intensity. Intensity is the magnitude of force or energy which is determined by the extent of displacement of molecules in the vibrator or medium. Intensity can be measured in two ways: either in sound pressure, or in microwatts. If one talks about intensity in terms of microwatts he is talking about the force or power of the sound. If, on the other hand, he describes intensity in terms of sound pressure level, he is describing sound in terms of its pressure aspects against something standing in the path of the sound. A microwatt then, is a measurement of force moving outward, and sound pressure is a measurement of force applied against a unit of area. It is quite interesting to note that sound pressure is proportional to the square root of the power of sound expressed in microwatts, and that therefore the pressure of a sound is proportional to the square root of the power of a sound. These relationships will be discussed in much greater detail in the unit dealing with intensity. Let us reiterate that the term loudness is the perceptual attribute of amplitude. "The term loudness is used to designate the magnitude of sensation experienced by an auditor when sound waves impinge on the ear drum" (4). The relationship between amplitude and loudness is nonlinear. Suffice it to say at this time that a tone of 1000 cycles per second is audible at a lower intensity than any tone of greater or lesser frequency and that, measuring from a "normal threshold of audibility" which has been established, loudness may be expressed in terms of "jnd" 's (just noticeable differences) (5). The decibel (abbreviated dB) is an expression of the relative intensities of two sounds. This relationship will be studied further in Part Two.

Let us recapitulate. We have discussed the conditions necessary for the production of wave motion. There must be a medium in which a wave can be transmitted. This medium must be elastic, containing particles which are capable of returning to a position of rest after being disturbed. The medium must consist of a mass which may be any source capable of vibratory motion. Any form of matter, then, such as solids, liquids, or gases is capable of conducting wave motion. In the absence of matter sound cannot be conducted, therefore sound does not travel through a vacuum nor through interplanetary space in which there is no atmosphere. The medium in which sound is transmitted is a three dimensional one, and sound travels spherically through that three dimensional medium. The medium is continuous and homogeneous in composition. Sound is created as a result of a disturbance of the molecules or particles in the medium as a result of the action of some sort of vibrator. These disturbances result in changes in pressure in the medium. When the vibrator moves in an outward direction, there is increased pressure brought to bear on the molecules adjacent to the vibrator in the medium. The increased pressure on the particles results in a state of "condensation" or "compression." The direction of the movement of the particles of the medium has been determined by the action of the vibrator. When the vibrator moves outward, the molecules of the medium move outward. As soon as the vibrator begins to move in the other direction, or back inward, the molecules of the medium are moved in that direction. The particle moves from its position of rest in one direction or another. The particle has limitations on the distance it can travel from the position of rest. These limitations are governed by the amount of elasticity of the medium. It is interesting to note that the molecules of the medium never actually touch one another, in spite of the fact that they may move close to one another as a result of the condensation or compression enacted by the vibrator. The molecules are unable to touch one another because of the atomical relationships between them. Electro-chemically this status would be known as the state of "polarity" in which the molecules are found.

MOLECULES IN COMPRESSION WAVE

MOLECULES IN RAREFACTION WAVE

FIGURE 4. (a) Molecules in a Wave of Compression. (b) Molecules in a Wave of Rarefaction. (From Judson and Weaver, *Voice Science,* 1942, by permission of Appleton-Century-Crofts, Inc.)

As soon as the vibrator moves in the opposite direction from that first observed, the molecules are more or less sucked along behind it, and the molecules of the medium are spread further apart. When they are spread further apart, there is a decrease of pressure upon each molecule. The state of decreased pressure is known as "rarefaction." Remember that the amount of displacement of the molecules of the medium has been determined by the elasticity of the medium. The particle is returned to its position of rest by the elasticity of the medium, and then is carried beyond its position of rest by the force of inertia operating within the medium. These relationships of compression and rarefaction are observed in Figure 4. Once a molecule is carried by the force of inertia past its position of rest, it is restored to the position of rest once more by the elasticity of the medium. These disturbances result in the displacement of particles in the medium.

We can perhaps obtain a better idea of the distance relationships between molecules if we were to perform the following bit of mathematical trickery. Let us assume that the distance a molecule is moved forward from its position of rest represents not direction forward but direction upward. Let us further assume that the distance a molecule travels backward from its position of rest will be represented as not backward movement, but rather downward. If we then trace out the distance relationships that molecules have moved from their positions of rest, we will have a graph which appears to be a curve identified mathematically as a "sine" wave. What we have actually done in transposing our understanding of the direction of movement of the molecules so that we are now discussing up and down movement rather than forward and backward, is to have made a transition from a longitudinal wave such as sound, to a horizontal wave such as water. The only reason for performing such mathematical trickery is to obtain a better understanding of the distance relationships between molecules and an understanding of how a wave moves outward from its source.

We can look at this sine wave and discuss various characteristics which it possesses. The upper half of a sine wave, which actually then would represent molecules moving forward from their positions of rest, is identified as the "crest" of the wave. The same wave form also displays a lower half with molecules moving backward from their positions of rest, which is identified as the "trough." The crest of the wave, as we usually observe this representation, has to do with molecules moving forward from their positions of rest, and the trough of the wave, as we ordinarily represent this, has to do with molecules moving backward from their positions of rest.

Now let us turn our attention to the matter of velocity. The velocity of molecules operating in a medium depends upon the composition of the medium. The more solid the medium, the faster the movement of the molecules which compose it. Velocity then, depends upon the composition of the medium, and there are three factors within the medium which determine the velocity. The first of these is density, the second is elasticity and the third is temperature. The greater the density of the medium, the slower the velocity of the wave being transmitted. This would mean that

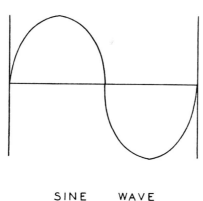

SINE   WAVE

FIGURE   5. A sine wave.

sound would travel much more slowly in solids than in gases, were it not for the fact that density is actually a minor factor in the determination of velocity. Far more important is the role of elasticity. The greater the elasticity in the medium the more rapid the transmission of the wave. There is much greater elasticity in solids, than in liquids, than in gases. This is the reason that sound can travel much more quickly through solid objects than it can through liquids, and travel much more swiftly through liquids than it can in gaseous states. We must also keep in mind that when we describe molecules as being at rest they actually are never so. Molecules of any medium are actually in constant motion. Molecules are traveling through a kind of three dimensional arc around a position in which they tend to remain, and stay relatively the same distance apart while exhibiting such motion. Particles in motion exhibit an oscillating movement as the wave is propagated through the medium.

The third factor having to do with the determination of velocity of the wave is the temperature of the medium. As temperature in-increases the molecules become less dense, and the velocity increases. As temperature decreases, molecules become more dense, and there is a decrease in the velocity with which the wave is propagated. As soon as molecules of the medium are spread further apart, as they do when they are made warmer, the density of the medium is lessened, and the velocity increases.

There is an interesting relationship between the velocity of the wave and the frequency of a sound being produced. Since velocity tends to be rather standard in a medium, that is, the velocity of sound in air tends to be always about the same, or the velocity of sound in water tends to be always about the same, or the velocity in steel tends always to be about the same, it is obvious that the space occupied by each cycle of vibration will change as the frequency of vibration changes. Actually the length of a sound wave in air is determined by the number of disturbances in the molecules of air which occur in one second. The number of disturbances per second results in a certain distance occurring be-

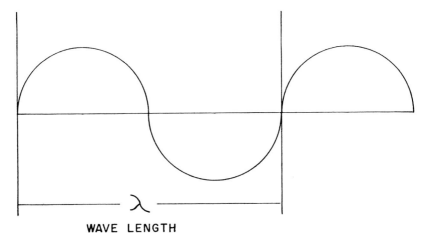

WAVE LENGTH

FIGURE 6. The determination of one wave length. (Reprinted with permission from Culver, *Musical Acoustics,* 4th ed., 1956, McGraw-Hill Book Co.)

tween a period of condensation, rarefaction, then another condensation, followed by another rarefaction, etc. This distance occupied by a cycle of a sound wave is referred to as "wave length" and the wave length is measured from any given point on a sine curve to any corresponding point on the curve of the next wave. It is then, for example, the distance from the molecule exhibiting the greatest displacement forward to the next molecule observed moving the greatest distance forward. Or it is the distance from the molecule exhibiting the greatest movement backward to the next molecule exhibiting the greatest movement backward. It is the distance, as a further example, from the crest of any one wave to the crest of the next, or from the trough of any one wave to the trough of the next.

There is a formula for determining this wave length. This formula is sometimes referred to as the "space equation." The space equation simply indicates that lambda (wave length) equals V÷F. Translated, this means that the wave length equals the velocity with which sound is traveling through the medium divided by the frequency of vibration. It so happens that sound movement through air has a velocity of about 1089 feet per second at 20° centigrade or 70° Fahrenheit. This is ordinarily rounded off for ease in handling, to 1100 feet per second.

If a vibrator were to vibrate at 1100 cycles per second, we can see that sound traveling at 1100 feet per second with a vibration occurring 1100 times per second would mean that each cycle of vibration would occupy one foot of space. Putting this relationship into the form of an equation, we emerge with the equation that wave length equals 1100 feet per second divided by 1100 cycles per second. Since we are expressing velocity in feet per second, the answer will be expressed in feet. Making the proper division then, we see that 1100 divided by 1100 equals 1 and the wave length of this particular example will be 1 foot. Let us take another example. Knowing that velocity remains essentially the same in air, except when there is a temperature difference, we can see that sound will have a relatively constant velocity around 1100 feet per second. Suppose that the vibrator were vibrating now at a rate of 2200 times per second, and the question were asked "How much space is occupied by each vibration?" Using our space equation, we would see that the wave length of each cycle would equal 1100 feet per second divided by 2200 cycles per second. Making the proper division, then, we emerge with the figure 1/2 foot. This tells us that the amount of space occupied by each cycle in this particular frequency would be 1/2 foot or 6 inches. We can use the same formula to determine the wave length of any frequency. The speed of sound in water is about 4700 feet per second, so each wave length is about four times longer in water than in air.

We can also use the space equation in another fashion. If we know the wave length of a given sound, we can determine the frequency of vibration. In this case we would make some simple arithmetic transformations of the equation and emerge with an equation of this form: Frequency equals velocity divided by wave length. If we knew, for example, that a certain sound had a wave length of 8 inches, we could determine the frequency. Our equation would be frequency equals 1100 feet per second divided by 8 inches, which equals 2/3 feet. Mathematically, we could then determine the frequency by either multiplying 1100 feet per second times 3/2, or by dividing 1100 feet per second by .67 feet. In either case, the frequency will be 1650 cycles per second.

Thus far as we have discussed the propagation of a sound wave, we have made no mention of the fact that sometimes the sound wave does not travel quite as easily as might be desirable. We have indicated that sound waves emanate from a source equally in all directions. A sound wave, then, travels spherically from the source of vibration. The spherical movement grows so rapidly, however, that as soon as the sound wave has traveled some 6 to 8 feet from the source, it is generally no longer regarded as spherical but as a plane wave. This simply indicates that the sphere has now become so large that as you look along the direction of movement of any one set of molecules, you see no curvature. A spherical wave is one in which any of the characteristic disturbances or displacements of any wave are the function of the radius and will be the distance measured to the wave front from the source of origin (6).

There are certain things that can interfere with the transmission of sound waves. The first of these is the factor known as reflection. A sound wave impinging upon any kind of a surface results in part of the wave being reflected, and part of the wave being absorbed. The smoother the surface which the sound strikes, the more energy which will be reflected, and the less absorbed. The rougher the surface which the sound strikes, the less reflected, and the more absorbed. There are actually two types of reflected sound waves. Diffuse reflection occurs when the wave length of the sound is comparable to the irregularities of the surface on which it is reflecting (usually very short wave lengths of high frequency sounds). In this circumstance, the sound wave more or less breaks up into many reflections of sound. The other type

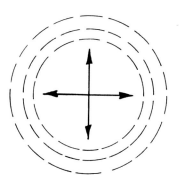

SPHERICAL WAVE

FIGURE   7. A spherical wave—sound as it emerges from the vibrator before any obstacles are encountered.

of reflection is termed regular reflection. It results from smooth surfaces and has the following characteristics. The angle of the reflected ray, the ray which bounces back from the surface, is equal to the angle of the ray hitting the surface. The latter ray is termed the incident ray. These angles are measured from an imaginary line which bisects the two angles and is perpendicular to the reflecting surface. This is expressed in Figure 8. The percentage of energy which will be reflected depends upon the type of surface. Solid surfaces, such as a plastered wall, reflect up to 100 per cent of the energy of the wave, thus giving maximum

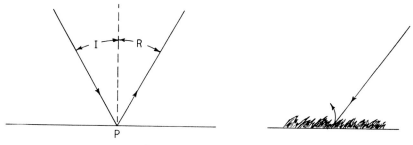

REFLECTION   OF   SOUND

FIGURE   8. Reflection of sound from a smooth surface and a rough surface. Little sound is reflected from a rough surface. (Reprinted with permission from Culver, *Musical Acoustics,* 4th ed., 1956, McGraw-Hill Book Co.)

reflection. Porous surfaces such as that used in sound proofing give a minimum of reflection, sometimes approaching as low as zero per cent. Keep in mind that any time a sound wave strikes a surface, part of the energy of the wave will be reflected and part of it will be absorbed. Reflection gives rise to echoes which indicate a brief period of reflection which is not sustained. Reflection which is prolonged or continuous results in reverberation. This produces a blurred sound effect, unintelligible speech and unintelligible music. It is also, interestingly enough, one of the prime techniques now being used in recording popular music.

As soon as one notes that reflection plays a role in transmission of sound, he faces the fact that there may now be several sound waves traveling through the same medium at the same time. As soon as this happens, then the same portion of the medium is transmitting any number of different wave series simultaneously. The waves then will have an effect upon one another. The waves are superimposed upon one another. If two waves are passing through a medium in the same direction at the same time, or in opposite directions, one wave is superimposed upon the other. If the waves passing in the same direction are in phase (and more regarding phase will be discussed later) the result is an upward and downward displacement equal to the algebraic sum of the displacement of each separate sound wave. If the sound waves are in phase, and the crests of both sounds coincide, the crest of the resultant wave will be much larger, the amplitude will be much greater, than that of each wave separately. The energy or intensity has been increased, which is the physical expression of the resultant change; one could also state that there will be a concomitant increase in loudness, which would be the statement dealing with the reaction or psychological impression to the change

FIGURE   9. Building up a complex wave: (a), (b) and (c) are sinusoidal components of different frequencies. Portion (a) has five times and portion (b) three times the frequency of portion (c). Portion (d) is the nonsinusoidal sum of (a), (b) and (c). (Reprinted with permission from Denes and Pinson, *The Speech Chain*, 1963, Bell Telephone Laboratories.)

in sound. Such a change is best shown when the two waves have the same frequency and are in phase.

If two waves are passing through the medium in opposite di-

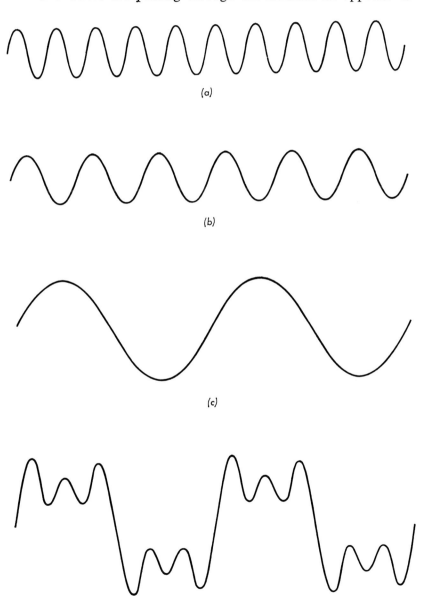

(a)

(b)

(c)

(d)

rections, the result will be a reduction in their amplitude equal to their algebraic sum. The point at which the forces oppose is known as a node. This point represents zero displacement. The

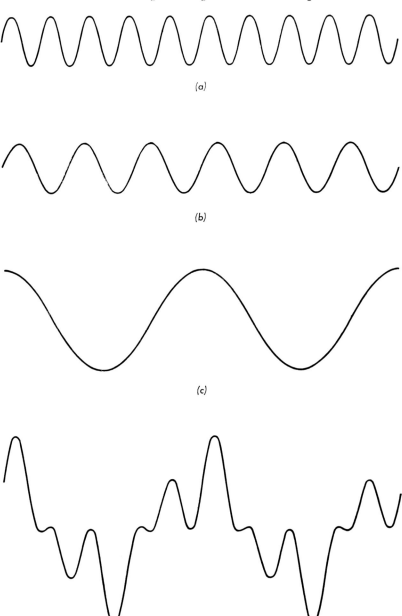

(a)

(b)

(c)

(d)

point of maximum displacement is called an antinode. If the waves have the same frequency and intensity they are known as standing or stationary waves. The neutralization of these two equal opposing forces results in silence even though the energy from the two vibrators is present.

Two sound waves passing thorugh the same medium simultaneously at different frequencies, intensities and phase produce a third type of wave. The point of opposing forces or intersecting forces is known as a beat. Beats are caused by alternative "additive" and "substractive" interference. Two waves arriving at any given point out of phase by one-half a period cause almost complete destructive interference. The interference lasts only a fraction of a second, causing the sound to appear continuous and vary only in intensity. The number of beats produced or heard is equal to the difference in the frequencies of the two primary sounds. Beats distinguish between two notes which differ from one another by only a few cycles per second. If there are more than sixteen beats per second, we hear no beats at all. Instead we hear a new tone, the "difference tone." Let us look at some examples of beats and difference tones. If two frequencies are present in a medium, one at 400 cycles per second, and the other at 405 cycles per second, what we actually hear will be the difference between these two frequencies. The difference, in this case, is 5 cycles per second. Since the ear is not capable of resolving a sound of this low a frequency into a single tone, we then hear these 5 cycles per second as individual events. In other words we will hear some type of sound which occurs 5 times within one second. This is actually the meaning of the term beat. If the two frequencies involved, for another example, were 400 cycles per second and 425 cycles per second, then we would once again hear the difference between the two sounds. Since the difference

FIGURE 10. The same component waves as shown in Figure 9, but with the phase of Figure 9 (c) changed; the resulting waveform has changed as shown in the (d) portion of this figure. (Reprinted with permission from Denes and Pinson, *The Speech Chain*, 1963, Bell Telephone Laboratorics.)

in this case is now 25 cycles per second, we have now reached the point where the ear is capable of resolving the difference into a single continuous tone. The tone we hear then will be a very low tone with a frequency of 25 cycles per second.

Whenever we hear beats, then, we are dealing with a frequency which is vibrating a lesser number of times per second than the ear is capable of interpreting as a single tone. The human ear is capable of hearing tones ranging from somewhere around 20 cycles per second to somewhere around 20,000 cycles per second. As soon as we deal with a frequency of less than 20 cycles per second, we are into the area of beats.

At the other end of the frequency scale which the human ear can interpret—as soon as we are dealing with a frequency greater than some 20,000 cycles per second—we are into the realm of "ultra-sonics" or "super-sonics" which deal with frequencies too high for the ear to perceive. One example of frequencies of this character is the simple dog whistle, with which most of us have had some experience. A child blows a whistle, which we do not hear, and a dog comes running to his master. Therefore we can make the safe assumption that a dog is capable of hearing frequencies too high for the human ear to perceive. Another example of ultra-sonic sound, which is becoming quite important, is the use of such frequencies as cleansing agents. Many instruments are now available for use in hospitals to cleanse medical instruments by ultra-sonic sound. In this type of instrument, a wave generator produces a sound somewhere in the neighborhood of 35,000 to 40,000 cycles per second. This sound is not perceived by the human ear, but the vibrations of such a sound through water produce such rapid vibratory actions of the water that medical instruments placed into such a water bath are vibrated extremely rapidly shaking loose foreign particles which cling to the instruments. Many hospitals are now using this type of cleansing agent.

We have also probably read or discussed at one time or another the use of ultra-sonics in surgery where a sound wave with a very high frequency, somewhere in the neighborhood of 40,000 to 50,000 cycles per second, is directed by a precise technique to a localized area of tissue. The sound wave is capable of producing such rapid vibratory motion in the tissue that the tissue is essentially destroyed. The major use of this type of surgical intervention has been in the province of neurosurgery in the brain.

The second kind of interference with a sound wave is refraction. Refraction has to do with the bending of a sound wave away from its path of propagation. It occurs when the determinants of velocity in the medium vary from one section of the medium to another. As will be evident, sound waves traveling through the atmosphere will be bent either toward or away from the ground depending upon the temperature of the ground compared to the temperature of the air. A sound wave is refracted toward the region of greater concentration of the medium, or, in other words, from hotter to colder air, hot water to cold water, hot metal to cold metal. If the layer of air near the ground is colder than the layer of air above the ground, sound waves will be refracted toward the surface of the ground.

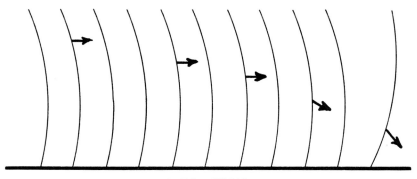

REFRACTION

FIGURE 11. The refraction of sound waves—sound being bent toward the ground. (Reprinted with permission from Culver, *Musical Acoustics,* 4th ed., 1956, McGraw-Hill Book Co.)

We have discussed the concept of reflection of sound, and indicated at the same time that some of the sound is always absorbed. Absorption of sound is the result of the dissipating of energy which results from forces set up by the air as it flows through small pores in some material. The ideal absorbing material is a flat porous surface with numerous small openings, such as our "acoustical tile." A material in which the small pores are not all

the same size is capable of trapping sounds with differing frequencies or wave lengths. A second good absorber of sound is
felt. Felt surfaces absorb up to 100 per cent of the sound. Many
of us are also familiar with the use of heavy curtains or drapes
to curtail the reflection of sound. If we have a room in a home
which reflects too much sound, we can use heavy curtains at the
windows to absorb some of the sound and reduce the problem of
reflection. The very first type of acoustical treatment available
back in the 1930's in radio stations, for example, was the use of
velvet draperies before there was such a thing as acoustical tile.

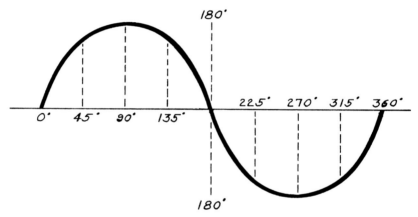

FIGURE 12. A graphic representation of phase. There are 360 degrees in
one complete cycle.

We mentioned earlier the concept of phase. Any aspect of our
existence which can be described by some kind of curve can also
be described in terms of phase. Phase is a kind of mathematical
means by which we look at various stages of production of a
sound, or of any other natural phenomenon which can be expressed via some type of curve. Since we have mentioned the use
of the sine wave as the graphical means by which sound may be
represented, we can divide that sine wave into sections. Each section can be divided off into a series of degrees of a circle. We
can then discuss the relationship between any one section of the
curve and any other section in terms of degrees, and this is the
meaning of the term phase.

Phase is the portion of a cycle through which a vibrator has passed in a given instant, or a portion of a wave compared to some other portion of a wave, and is expressed in terms of degrees of a circle. Sounds are said to be in phase at any given instant when their degree of advancement from some arbitrary zero point is equal. If two waves are of equal frequency, they would be either in phase or out of phase throughout the duration of their vibration. If two sounds are in phase, they can be considered to be 0° out-of-phase. Most sounds, therefore, will be out-of-phase. They are out of phase whenever they are not precisely in-phase.

Turning to our graph in Figure 12, and remembering that a circle contains 360 degrees, we can see that the crest of a wave can be considered to be 180 degrees and the trough of the wave another 180 degrees. The distance from the base line, which could be considered to be the line in which molecules are exhibiting no displacement, or are found in their positions of rest, to the top of the crest, then, would represent a distance of 90 degrees. From the top of the crest to the base line again would represent an additional 90 degrees. The total distance then involved in the crest of the wave is 180 degrees. Likewise, from the base line, the line of zero displacement, to the bottom-most portion of the trough is an additional 90 degrees, and from the bottom-most position of the trough back to the base line is a final 90 degrees. By comparing any two sounds, or any two aspects of the same sound, in relationship to where molecules are from the base line moving along the direction of the circle, we can determine the phase relationships between the items in question.

We just indicated that different aspects of the same sound wave can be compared in terms of phase relationships. There are three aspects which we might compare. These are displacement, velocity and pressure. Let us first establish an arbitrary arrangement to indicate the displacement of molecules. This would probably be best accomplished with the assistance of the classroom instructor, and is also most helpful with the assistance of a sheet of graph paper. If one uses a sheet of graph paper in which there are 5 squares to the inch, he can, by holding the paper horizontally, and spacing molecules 3 spaces apart, indicate steps for 16 or 17 air molecules across the top of the paper. These molecules represent molecules in the medium before any disturbance by sound.

Then we can make some arbitrary judgments about the amount of displacement which would be incurred by these air molecules as the vibration disturbs their environment in the medium. Let us assume that molecules 4, 10, and 16 suffer the greatest displacement, and let us arbitrarily assign the amount of displacement as 4 positions, 4 squares backward and forward from the position of rest. Molecules 4 and 16, then, would be moved forward from their postions of rest, and molecule 10 moved backward from its postion of rest. To obtain a smooth-looking curve, let us further assume that molecules 2, 6 and others in a series will be displaced 2 squares forward and backward from their positions of rest, and that molecules 3, 5 and others in that same pattern be displaced 3-1/2 squares forward or backward from their positions of rest. After making these assumptions, and drafting a line in which displacement forward is represented by movement above the line and displacement backward represented by displacement below the line, we emerge with a graph quite similar to that shown in Figure 13. We now have a graphic representation of particle displacement at some instant in time. The base line along which are located molecules 1, 7 and 13, indicates molecules which at this particular instant in time are located in, and passing through, their positions of rest.

The last statement provides us with an interesting piece of information. If we now turn our attention to the velocity of the air molecules, we note that a molecule in moving from its position of rest actually slows down as it approaches the limit of its excursion in either direction from that position of rest, since it ceases movement and begins to move in the opposite direction. In other words, a molecule moves forward from its position of rest to a certain point, actually stops, begins to move in the opposite direction to a certain point, where it once again stops and moves forward through its position of rest once more. The important aspect to grasp here is that molecules will actually be traveling fastest as they move through their positions of rest moving from one direction to the other. Since this is the case, molecules will have greatest velocity at the point in our graph of displacement which actually represents zero displacement, or molecules being found in their positions of rest.

Let us then draw another graph, which shall be called a graphic representation of particle velocity at some given instant in time. If we use the same arbitrary decision about extent of placement of molecules above and below the line, we establish the principle that molecules moving fastest will be located four spaces above or below the line, and that the line this time shall represent no velocity or zero velocity. We shall also recognize the fact that such a nomenclature for a line is actually not accurate, since all mole-

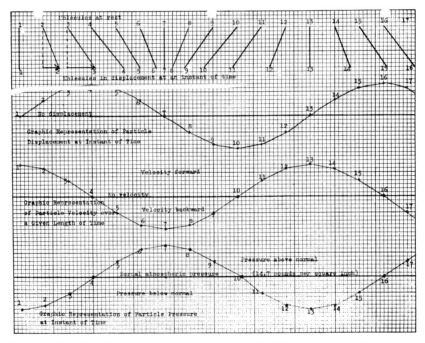

FIGURE 13. Graphic representation of particle displacement, velocity and pressure.

cules are exhibiting some movement at any time we select. Molecules 1, 7 and 13, which were found in our displacement graph to be located at their positions of rest, shall actually then be represented as having greatest velocity passing through the position of rest, and shall be located, in the case of molecules 1 and 13, four spaces above the line, and in the case of molecule 7, four spaces below the line. We can then, using our same arbitrary arrangement of placement, show that molecule 2 will be located three and one-half spaces above the line; molecule 3, located two spaces above the line; molecule 4, located on the line; molecule 5, located two spaces below the line; molecule 6, located three and one-half spaces below the line; molecule 7, located four spaces below the line, etc. Any molecule located above the line can be considered to be moving in a forward direction. Any molecule located beneath the line can be considered to be moving in a backward direction.

If we compare our graphic representation of displacement with that of velocity, we can note that some molecules which are located backward of their positions of rest are actually in the process of moving forward. Likewise, some molecules which are located forward of their positions of rest on our displacement graph, are actually in the process of moving backwards. We can now trace out the phase relationship between displacement and velocity. To do so, we simply ascertain how a molecule would have to be moved along our graphic representation of displacement to occupy the same space as it does on our graphic representation of velocity. If we use particle 1 as an example, we can see that on the displacement graph, particle 1 lies along the line of no displacement. In the velocity graph, however, molecule 1 is located four spaces above the line. If we place our finger upon molecule 1 on the displacement graph and begin to imaginarily move molecule 1 around the displacement graph until it occupies the same position upon that graph as it does on that of velocity, we are moving molecule 1 on the displacement graph 90 degrees. This means that displacement and velocity are out-of-phase by 90 degrees. To prove this, we simply take other molecules and perform the same operation with them as we have just done with molecule 1. In each case, we can see that a molecule must move 90 degrees around the displacement graph to occupy the same spot which it does upon the velocity graph.

We can now ascertain a graphic representation of particle pressure. Keep in mind that pressure upon the molecules can actually be divided into two stages; a stage of "condensation" or "compression," and a stage of "rarefaction." The molecules in the compression phase will be those molecules which have greater pressure placed upon them than is true when they occupy their positions of rest. The compression phase of a sound wave, then, is that in which molecules are squeezed together and are closer together than they are when undisturbed in the medium. If we then look back at our pattern of displacement to see which molecules, after being disturbed by a sound wave, are squeezed closer together, we note that molecules 4 and 16 are squeezed more tightly than are any other molecules. This means that molecules 4 and 16 would be located in the centers of the compression phases of the sound wave.

If we now attempt to draw another graph, and use as our base line molecules exhibiting normal (atmospheric) pressure, and use the same arbitrary arrangement of placement of molecules above and below the line, we shall place molecules 4 and 16 four spaces above the line. Everything above the line, in this case, illustrates molecules observed in the compression phase of the sound wave. Everything below the line would represent molecules observed in a rarefaction phase of the sound wave. Looking back at our displacement graph for molecules which are now spread out more than they were in their positions of rest, we note that molecule 10 now has greater room between itself and any other molecules. Molecule 10, then, will be located at the center of the rarefaction stage of a sound wave. We shall place molecule 10 four spaces below the line. Now by using our same arrangement of placement of molecules two spaces above and below the line, and three and one-half spaces above and below the line, we can enter the remainder of the air molecules in place on our graph to finish the graphic representation of particle pressure. Normal (atmospheric) pressure, by the way, is approximately 15 pounds per square inch, and we might desire to note this entry along our line which represents molecules found under normal atmospheric pressure. We can now compare phase relationships between displacement and pressure, and between velocity and pressure. When we do so, by the same process discussed earlier, we note that displacement and pressure are 90 degrees out-of-phase, and that velocity and pressure are exactly in phase.

Phase relationships involving pressure are more difficult to see. If one looks at molecule 7, for example, greatest velocity backward is observed, and greatest pressure is observed. Velocity and pressure are in-phase. The same relationship is established by looking at molecule 19 (if your graph contains that many). For molecules 1 and 13, however, greatest forward velocity is observed, but least pressure is seen. In spite of this fact, velocity and pressure are regarded as being in phase. One of the difficulties in understanding this clearly lies with our example. For the displacement and velocity graphs, the base line indicates no displacement and no velocity. For the pressure graph, however, the base line indicates normal (atmospheric) pressure.

During our earlier discussion of phase relationships, we mentioned that phase could be used not only to discuss the relationships between different aspects of the same sound being generated, but between different sounds. Consider, for example, the two pure tones represented in Figure 14. They both have the same frequency, but one begins upon the base line whereas the other begins at the maximum trough position. The phase relationship between

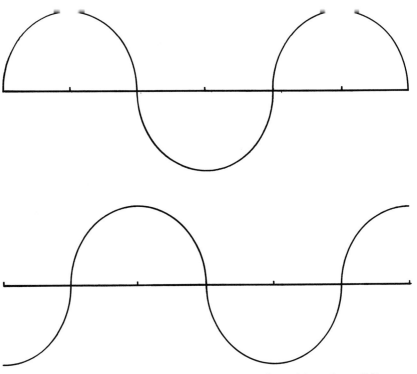

FIGURE 14. Two tones with the same frequency, but with a phase difference of ninety degrees.

the two tones is identical throughout the entire aspect of their wave travel. The second tone is at zero degrees when the first tone is at 90 degrees. There is a phase difference of 90 degrees between these two tones. This phase difference is constant because the two tones are the same frequency. Were these tones to have different frequencies, the phase relationships between them would be constantly changing, so that at some times the sounds might be 90 degrees apart in phase, sometimes 180 degrees, sometimes 240 degrees, sometimes 313, etc.

II

RESONANCE

A NOTHER ASPECT OF SOUND which is ordinarily quite confusing
to the student in Speech Pathology and Audiology with little background in high school or college physics is the concept of resonance. Resonance may be defined as the seeming amplification of
sound resulting from a reflection and concentration of sound waves
in such a manner that makes possible a considerable increase of
energy output of the vibrating agent in less time (7). The basic
idea to this definition is that resonators do not create energy:
rather, they release it or permit it to be expanded more rapidly
by the wave train with less resistance. A resonator is simply some
kind of tube or pipe or chamber of some size or another which
produces an effect upon a sound reaching it. Most tubes or pipes
or chambers have what is termed a "natural resonating frequency"
which in a sense enables frequencies which match those natural
resonant frequencies to pass through the chamber with relative
ease, and with all the energy present at those particular frequencies
to be liberated without difficulty.

Let us return once more to some of the ingredients necessary
for the production of sound. Resonance forms a kind of third
ingredient in the production of a sound. A sound is produced by
the action of some kind of generating source operating upon a
vibrator. The generating force is the energy necessary for a vibrator
to commence operation. The vibrator then is the actual source of
the sound. For example, a violinist takes a bow which is the generator and with that bow plucks a string on the violin. The string
of the violin vibrates, serves as the vibrator and produces a sound.
The generator, then, sets a vibrator into motion. We already know
that the number of times the vibrator moves back and forth in
one second determines the frequency of the sound being emitted
by the vibrator. Thus, a vibrator moving back and forth 250 times

per second emits a tone having a frequency of 250 cycles per second or Hertz. The resonator, now, is a second body set into vibration by the action of the first vibrator. For example, returning to the violin discussed above, the vibration of the violin string, the vibrator, sets the air in the box of the violin into vibration. This box of the violin, which contains air, is the resonator. A resonator gives out no tone unless impulses are received from some other vibrator which in turn is activated by a generator. If the generator supplies a vibration of the vibrator which has the same frequency as the natural resonating frequency of the resonator, the condition is described as "free vibration" of the resonator.

Different types of resonating bodies are capable of different types of resonance. Generally speaking, there are three types of resonance. One is termed sharp resonance, and obtains when the response of the resonator is maximum. This happens when the resonator and vibrator exactly agree in frequency. Sharp resonance then is simply another term for what was already described as "free vibration." The second type of resonance is called broad resonance. Such resonance obtains when the resonator responds to a wide range of frequencies, and so will respond to many vibrators. This will happen when the resonator does not have a particularly tuned natural resonating frequency. If we look at Figure 15, we can see a graphic description of the contrast between sharp and broad resonance in terms of the frequencies to which they respond and the way in which they respond to these various frequencies. The third type of resonance is termed sympathetic resonance. Such a resonance applies when one is dealing with more than one resonator. If different resonators have the same natural resonating frequency, a vibration of any one of the resonators will produce a similar reaction from the other resonators. For example, if the loud pedal of a piano is pressed, all of the strings are left free to vibrate. Now a singer begins to sing the scale, producing vibrations of his vocal folds. As each note is sung, tones will be produced by the strings of the piano whose vibrating frequencies correspond to the frequencies contained in the note which the individual sings.

This latter example takes us into a new area. When we say

that different strings of a piano vibrate at the same time in response to a note which an individual sings, we are informed that each note sung by an individual contains more than one frequency. When a tone to which we are listening contains more than one frequency, the tone is described as being complex. Pure tones are relatively

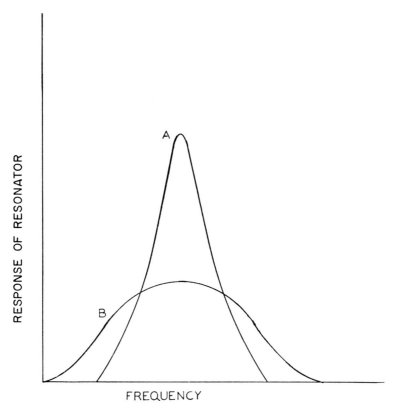

FIGURE 15. Sharp and broad resonance. Sharp resonance is represented by A, broad resonance by B. (Reprinted with permission from Culver, *Musical Acoustics,* 4th ed., 1956, McGraw-Hill Book Co.)

rare acoustic events in a person's normal environment. They are produced ordinarily only by some clinical or experimental investigator who is checking on relationships of a particular nature with a particular sound. The majority of sounds that we ordinarily hear, such as people talking, or car horns, or elevator noise, or the shuffling of feet on a floor, or the movement of chairs or tables, all of these are complex. That is to say, they involve at the same time more than one frequency. Vibrating structures that act as sources for such sounds, and are responsible for the creation of such sounds, do not vibrate in a sinusoidal manner, such as the sounds which we have described in the first section of this book. The wave forms of these vibrations do not look like sine waves. Back in the 19th century, a French mathematician, Fourier, demonstrated that any wave form repeating itself periodically, no matter how complex, can be broken into a series of sinusoids of different amplitudes, frequencies, and phases. There is a distinct relationship which obtains between these different sinusoids. Each of the sinusoids contained in a complex sound bears a mathematical relationship to the lowest frequency sinusoid present. This lowest frequency sound present in a complex sound is termed the "fundamental frequency." The fundamental frequency has a period which is equal to that of the entire complex sound. Examples of this relationship are shown in Figures 9 and 10. If one were to examine all the individual sine waves which compose a complex wave, then superimpose them upon one another, he could emerge with a picture of the original complex sound wave. This type of analysis is termed either Fourier analysis or harmonic analysis.

Harmonic analysis is performed at present with electronic instrumentation, but the basic principles have been known since the days of Helmholtz. In such an analyzer the idea is to gather together a whole group of mechanical resonators, each of which will respond to a given sound. A set of such resonators, as used by Helmholtz, consisted of distorted spheres enclosing different volumes of air depending upon their sizes. A full set of such analyzers would cover a wide range of frequencies. One then produces a complex sound to be analyzed and then notes which of these resonators is vibrating and to what degree of amplitude. This is the same type of process which we just described by singing a note close to the piano and looking inside to see which strings are vibrating or resonating in response to the note being sung. You then know, if you know the frequencies at which these different strings in the piano are set, the frequencies that are contained within the note being sung by the individual.

In the empirical world about us, we generally encounter two different types of resonators. One of these is termed a mechanical resonator and the second an acoustical resonator. A mechanical resonator is any mechanical body free to vibrate having a natural period of oscillation. Since it has a natural period of oscillation, which corresponds to the natural resonating frequency, it is therefore capable of being a resonator. For example, if a mass is fastened at one end, and has the other end free, as in Figure 16, it will

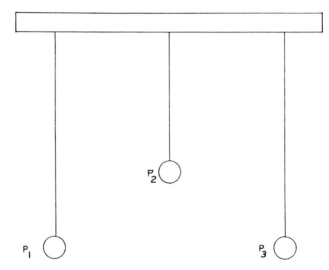

FIGURE 16. Pendulums illustrating mechanical resonance. (Reprinted with permission from Culver, *Musical Acoustics,* 4th ed., 1956, McGraw-Hill Book Co.)

vibrate a certain number of times when the free end is pulled. This number of vibrations is known as its natural vibrating frequency or natural resonating frequency. This natural vibrating frequency, which would be reciprocal to the natural vibrating period, is determined by many factors depending upon the individual object. In the case of a bottle, the natural period depends upon the size of the cavity, the size of the opening, and the length of the neck of the bottle. As another example, let us re-examine the situation shown in Figure 16. Here three pendulums are suspended from a common board. Pendulum 1 and pendulum 3 have the same length and mass, the same length being the distance of the wire connecting them to the board. Since they have the same mass and have wire of the same length connecting them to the board, they will have the same natural resonating period. Pendulum 2 is shorter, that is, it is not suspended as far from the board by its wire, therefore will have a different vibrating period. When pendulum 1 vibrates, pendulum 3 will also vibrate, but pendulum 2 will remain in its rest position. As a further example of mechanical resonance, we can take two tuning forks which are adjusted to the same frequency. If these are mounted on a common base, and one is struck, the second will also begin to vibrate.

The second kind of resonator we encounter is an acoustical resonator. An acoustical resonator simply consists of something that contains gas or air. This container filled with air will respond similarily to a mechanical body. For example, a man using a whistle is using acoustical resonance. The rush of air through the mouthpiece actually make a pretty feeble sound. If that rush of air, however, has the same natural resonating frequency as the air within the cavity of the whistle, resonance occurs, and the sound seems much louder. As another example, let us look at Figure 17, where a flask or bottle partially filled with water sits on a table. The flask or glass or bottle is actually partially filled with water and partially filled with air. Now if a tuning fork is brought near that flash, and the tuning fork is struck, a sound will be given off from the part of the flask filled with air. Actually one may experiment with this type of acoustical resonating device, beginning with an empty flask (one completely filled with air), use different tuning forks, begin slowly filling part of the flask with water, and continuing to use different tuning forks, may find levels of the water, and consequently levels of the air, at which different tuning forks are resonated.

The simplest type of acoustical resonator is a tube resonator of which there are two basic types. One is called a closed tube resonator, where one end is closed and the other end is open, such as a glass or a milk bottlc. With this type resonator, the tube resonates to a tone which has a wave length 4 times the length of the tube. For example, let us suppose that a glass is 4 inches high. To what frequency will it resonate best? The first question is to ascertain which frequency has a wave length that would be

4 times 4 inches or 16 inches. Sixteen inches is equal to 1 and 1/3 feet. Now we revert to the space equation, in which we learn that wave length equals velocity divided by frequency, and establish an equation which says 1 and 1/3 feet equals 1100, the velocity of sound in air, divided by frequency. By transposition, we ascertain that frequency will equal 1100 times 3/4. Solving the equation gives us the answer that frequency will be 825 cycles per second.

The second type of tube resonator is that termed the open tube, where both ends of the tube are open, such as a section of hollow pipe or a vibraphone duct. This type tube resonator resonates to a tone which has a wave length 2 times the length of the tube. For example, let us suppose that a piece of copper tubing, open

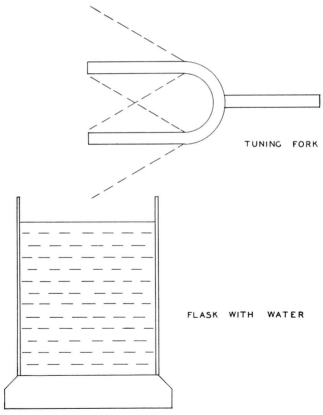

TUNING FORK

FLASK WITH WATER

FIGURE 17. Flask and tuning fork illustrating acoustical resonance. (Reprinted with permission from Culver, *Musical Acoustics*, 4th ed., 1956, McGraw-Hill Book Co.)

at both ends, is 7 inches long. And the question again is asked to what frequency will the tube resonate best? This time, which frequency has a wave length that is two times 7 inches or 14 inches? Fourteen inches equal 1 and 1/6 feet. Reverting to the space equation one more, we say 1 and 1/6 feet equals 1100, the velocity of sound in air, divided by frequency. By transposition, that frequency will equal 1100 times 6/7. Solving the equation gives us the answer of 943 cycles per second.

We should also refer to the idea of coupling, which occurs when two or more resonators, each capable of resonance, are joined together. When any part of the system vibrates, force will be exerted on the other parts of the system and they will also vibrate. Coupling is a very important aspect of resonance in the human voice, since resonance is dependent upon the travel of air through all the resonating chambers in the vocal tract, all of which are joined together. A loosely coupled system is one in which the force that any part of the system exerts on other parts of the system is small. A tightly coupled system, on the other hand, is one in which the force that one part of the system exerts on other parts is great.

The damping factor was mentioned earlier, and shown in Figure 1. Damping always occurs in resonance. It is the name applied to the phenomenon that a vibrator always vibrates for a shorter period of time when a resonator is attached to it, or when an object vibrates along with it. The period of time that a vibrator vibrates is called the period of vibration. Do not confuse the concept of period of vibration with the term "period" which was introduced earlier. The factor of damping simply indicates that any time resonance is involved, the period of vibration of a vibrator is reduced. When a tuning fork is struck with average force let us say that it vibrates for "X" seconds. If a resonator is held near the fork, the sound appears to be louder and can be heard further away, but the fork will vibrate for less than "X" seconds. It must be understood that whenever a vibrator is involved, toward the end of vibration movement involved is very minimal, and probably cannot be detected with the human eye. Therefore, sometimes it is difficult to establish actual temporal differences in the length of time of vibration when resonance is present and when it is not present. However, if movement of a vibrator were analyzed under a high powered microscope, so that each vibration could be observed, then the presence of damping would be much more evident. The reason that a sound appears louder when a resonator is present is that energy of the vibrator is radiated much faster or dissipated much more quickly. The amplitude of the vibrations from the vibrator is decreased faster than is the case when a resonator is not present. Every resonator has some damping effect on the period of vibration of the vibrator.

Let us now turn our attention to the factor of resonance in the human voice. Let us first recapitulate some earlier statements. A generator, which in this case will be air from the lungs during the process of expiration, forces a vibrator to vibrate. The vibrator in the human vocal tract is the vocal folds in the larynx. These vocal folds are vibrated by the stream of air coming from the lungs. Since the vocal folds are a rather complex mass of tissue, some differential pattern of vibration is observed whenever they move. Let us say that not all sections of the vocal folds move exactly to the same degree at exactly the same time. Some parts begin movement slightly before other parts, some parts do not move as rapidly as other parts, etc. The result of this differential movement in the vocal folds is the production of a complex tone, as opposed to a pure tone. Since a complex tone is produced by the vocal folds, and since the complex tone is composed of a fundamental frequency and some other sinusoids, the effect is to produce not only the fundamental frequency but also some overtones by the vibrations of the vocal folds. The human vocal resonance system is made up of irregularly shaped cavities, with a variety of hard and soft surfaces linked together in a relatively complex manner. We are sure that there are at least five different portions of the resonating cavity system in the human vocal tract; the laryngeal cavity (the space above the vocal folds), the ventricle of the larynx (a small side chamber departing from each side of the space between the vocal folds and ventricular folds in the larynx), the pharyngeal cavity (which itself is divided into three portions; the laryngo-pharynx, the oro-pharynx and the naso-pharynx), the oral cavity and the nasal cavity. The space above the vocal folds, otherwise termed the supra-glottic area, is a small space with rather soft walls on all sides. The ventricle of the larynx is an extremely small space, again with relatively soft walls surrounding it. The pharynx is a long, somewhat tube-like resonator with soft side and rear walls which are moved toward the center and back away from the center by means of muscular action. The front of the tube is irregular, made of soft tissue and muscular structure of varying shapes. The upper portion of the pharynx opens into the oral and nasal cavities. The presence of the tonsilar tissue and the size of such tissue compared to the size of the opening from the oro and naso-pharynx are important factors in the resonance functions of the pharynx. Sometimes adenoidal or tonsilar tissue can obstruct the opening into the naso-pharynx and nasal cavities, thereby changing speech resonance. The nasal cavity is the upper most part of the resonating system. The nasal cavity is open at the front and back, but is divided by a vertical bone and cartilaginous wall in mid-line, described as the nasal septum. At the rear of the cavity, the side walls are bony with thin tissue coverings subject to swelling which will affect resonance. Persons who are subject to chronic post nasal drip will attest to this characteristic in their voices. One will also observe such reactions in persons who have a long standing sinus difficulty. Toward the rear portion of the cavity, on each side, there are three small turbinate bones, which are actually bony protrusions into the cavity space. Ordinarily the nasal cavity as a resonator is a relatively set resonator, that is, little change in shape or size is ordinarily encountered. Such changes that are encountered are those produced by the discharge of material in sinus difficulty, or allergy, etc., an involvement of the soft tissue in the rear portion of the nasal cavity. It is possible in a normal operating vocal mechanism to close the nasal cavity off to some degree from the rest of the system, so that it poses little import in the production of certain sounds. The device by which this is accomplished is movement of the soft palate up to the posterior pharyngeal wall, essentially blocking air from going into the nasal cavity. It is important to realize that such blockage never occurs completely, and that there is always some air which goes into the nasal cavity. Generally speaking, in the production of all speech sounds except the nasal sounds [m], [n] and [ŋ], little air moves into the nasal cavity past the so-called closed soft palate.

The oral cavity is the most variable of the resonance chambers in the human vocal system. We can adjust the size and shape of the cavity by dropping the jaw, by moving the tongue around, by movement of the lips and by puffing of the cheeks. In size, shape and sound reflecting or absorbing surfaces, the oral cavity is the most variable of the speech resonance chambers.

There are probably two important ways in which the resonators act during the production of speech. First, vowels are formed by adjustments in the resonance characteristics of the oral cavity and the oro-pharynx. The raising and lowering of the jaw affects changes in the oral opening. The location of the hump of the tongue divides the cavity into resonance areas, and the position and shaping of the lips control the anterior opening and length of the cavity in front of the tongue hump. These adjustments create resonance conditions for the vowels which will be discussed later. Secondly, voice quality is partially determined by the sizes, shapes, coupling and tensions in the resonance system. The matter of resonance in voice quality will also be discussed later. The relative intensities of various overtones which are present as the tone is produced in the vocal folds can be changed considerably by the action of these different cavities. If a "throat microphone," such as that used by bomber pilots during World War II which is placed right on the hump of the "Adam's apple" on the larynx, is used, and the pick-up from that microphone analyzed, by far the strongest component of a sound produced will be the fundamental frequency of vibration of the vocal folds. Other sounds present will be the overtones also produced by the action of the vibration of the vocal folds. Now if another microphone were placed in a standard position out in front of the lips of the individual, and the output of this microphone also analyzed, great changes in the relative amplitude or intensity of different frequencies will be observed. The fundamental frequency generally will no longer be the strongest component present in the complex tone. Some of the overtones will now have achieved much more prominence, in terms of intensity, than the original fundamental frequency. Such a phenomenon is simply indicative of the importance of resonance in the human vocal system, and the output of that system.

III

VOCAL FREQUENCY

W E HAVE STATED EARILER that the fundamental frequency in the human voice is produced by the action of the vocal folds. The vocal folds are folds of ligament, muscle and mucous membrane that extend from the apex of the thyroid cartilage in front to the arytenoid cartilages at the back. The space between the vocal folds is called the glottis. When the arytenoids, and therefore, the vocal folds, are pressed together the air passage is cut off and the laryngeal valve is shut. The glottal opening is controlled basically by moving the arytenoids together and apart as they sit atop the cricoid cartilage. The open glottis is shaped somewhat like an arrow or a "v," as shown in Figure 18. The vocal folds are held together relatively closely at the front, and the greatest movement is seen in the rear portion of the vocal folds toward the arytenoid cartilages. The arytenoid cartilages are capable of two different types of movement, a gliding movement from center to side or vice versa, and a pivoting type of motion in which the lateral most edges of the arytenoid cartilages are pulled posteriorly, thus producing a pivoting action upon the central axis of the arytenoid cartilage. Both types of motion are controlled by muscle connections into the larynx. The glottis is about 3/4 of an inch long and the opening between the arytenoid cartilages ordinarily amounts to perhaps 1/4 to 1/2 inch.

When we talk, the vocal folds rapidly open and close. Each time the folds are closed, air pressure builds up beneath the folds and becomes strong enough to blow the folds apart. Once apart, this pressure is released, and the vocal folds return again to their closed position. Pressure builds up again, and the cycle repeats itself. The number of times per second that the vocal folds open and close yields the number of cycles per second of the fundamental frequency of vibration. This frequency is controlled by a combination of factors. We must consider the mass of the vocal folds, their tension and their length. There is also an effect produced by low air pressure created in the glottis by air from the sub-glottic area rushing through the narrow glottic opening into the wider air space of the supra-glottic area. The low air pressure

Vocal Folds

Top view

Front

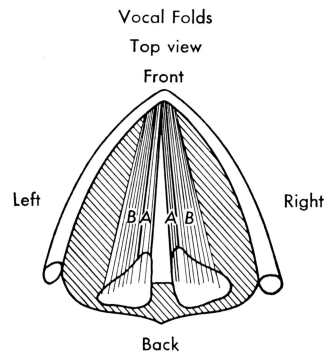

Left   Right

Back

FIGURE 18. A superior view of the vocal folds. The white space between the folds is the glottis. The black lines at the edges of the folds indicate the locations of the vocal ligaments. Next to the ligaments are the vocalis muscles (A). Next to the vocalis muscles are the thyroarytenoid muscles (B). (Reprinted with permission from Hanley and Thurman, *Developing Vocal Skills,* 1962, Holt, Rinehart and Winston, Inc.)

at the glottis produced by this rush of air into the supra-glottic space produces a sort of vacuum at the level of the glottis. This partial vacuum assists in drawing the vocal folds back to their starting position or closed position and increases the speed of the return. The more air pressure coming from the lungs, the more this effect is noted and the greater the number of vibrations per second. The theory of vocal production just outlined is termed the "myoelastic-aerodynamic" theory. Another theory of vocal vibration is termed the "neuro-chronaxic" theory, in which each vibration is enacted by a nerve impulse. Adherence to the neuro-chronaxic theory has been made difficult by recent reports by Von Leden and Moore (8) and Rubin (9), in which phonation has been shown not to occur when sub-glottic air pressure is absent, even though the nerve supply is kept intact. During speech, we are also able to continually adjust and alter tension and length of the vocal folds. The normal range of vocal fold frequencies encountered in a speaker amounts to about 1-1/2 octaves.

The frequency of vibration of the vocal folds is the actual number of vibrations or cycles that occur in one second. Pitch is our physchological interpretation of this frequency of vibration. Fletcher (10) has shown that amplitude of vibration and quality as well as frequency act to modify our sense of pitch. There is not a one to one relationship between frequency and pitch. One will recall that in the beginning chapter, relationships between pitch and frequency were discussed, pertinent to the Mel Scale of pitch. In spite of the fact that frequency and pitch are not the same phenomenon, we still speak in terms of pitch level and pitch range of a human voice, when we are actually referring to the frequency of vibration of the vocal folds and the range of frequencies which a given individual can produce.

During speech, the pitch level of a given individual varies throughout a wide range but in a period of time tends to distribute itself around a central or standard or habitual pitch level. We can actually speak of pitch level according to three classifications. Habitual pitch is that pitch level, determined by the frequency of vibration of the vocal folds, used most frequently by a given speaker (11). This level can be obtained by narrowing the range that a person speaks and gradually sustaining the voice in a vowel monotone. Pronovost (12) has discussed the method for finding the habitual pitch level of a speaker as follows:

> Investigation of the method for determining habitual pitch by narrowing the range gradually until the individual chants in a monotone, and then sustaining a vowel at the same pitch as the monotone, reveals

that the sustained tone tends to approximate the median pitch in superior speakers. Deviations from the median tend to be lower than the median, and did not exceed one tone in the present study. The method appears to be valid for determining the habitual pitch of superior speakers. Its use by the average speaker will depend somewhat upon his ability to narrow his range according to instruction.

The second classification is termed natural pitch level. The natural pitch level is that level determined by the characteristics of a particular speaker's mechanism wherein speech is most efficiently produced (13). Natural pitch level, then, is the pitch level which an individual should use in terms of his physiological equipment. There are at least five different methods for determining the natural pitch level. Pronovost (14) lists these as follows:

1. The 25% method, which locates the natural pitch level 25% of the way up the total singing range *including* falsetto.
2. The 33% method, which locates the natural pitch level 33% of the way up the total singing range *excluding* falsetto.
3. The 38% method, which locates the natural pitch level 38% of the way up the total singing range *excluding* falsetto.
4. The "one musical third below the middle tone" method, which locates the natural pitch level one musical third (two tones) below the middle note of the normal singing range *excluding* falsetto.
5. The five tones method, which locates the natural pitch level five tones above the lowest sustained tone.

In order to further understand how to find the natural pitch level, we should explain some terms used by Pronovost. We are probably all more or less familiar with the concept of falsetto voice production. When we are singing a scale and try to sing as high as we can, we reach a point where our voice no longer sounds like the same voice. If we sing high enough in pitch, we seem to reach a point where we change our voice completely. This is falsetto voice production. It is determined by the fact that the vocal folds change their mode of operation. In falsetto, the vocal folds no longer open and close along their entire length. Instead, enough tension is placed upon the vocal folds that they remain closed except for a small aperture at the anterior end of the vocal folds. The rapid vibration of that small aperture at the anterior end of the folds produces the very high frequency of vibration responsible for falsetto voice production. Ordinarily, an individual can produce

5 or 6 different notes, or roughly 2/3 of an octave, in his falsetto range.

The other concept which may require some explanation has to do with the relationship between frequency in terms of cycles per second and the term "tones." A tone is a musical term based upon the Equally Tempered Musical Scale, which was discussed earlier. The tone which serves as the base when the Equally Tempered Musical Scale is employed in speech research is the A above middle C at 440 cycles per second. When this A is the key value, the lowest tone in the scale, referred to as the "zero frequency level" or C_0, is 16.35 cycles per second. Consequently C_1, which would lie one octave above the zero frequency level, will have a frequency of 32.70 cycles per second. Proceeding upward along the musical scale, octave by octave, we finally encounter what we ordinarily refer to as middle C having a frequency of 261.60 cycles per second, and bearing the designation of C_4.

Other values of C are shown in Table I. Within each octave there are six whole tones and 12 semi-tones. This information is of value simply as information. A more pertinent interpretation of an octave is to say that it consists of 8 notes on the piano. Within

TABLE I

FREQUENCIES AND TONAL VALUES OF "C" MUSICAL NOTES

Note	Frequency (cps)	Tones above C_0	cps per Tone
C_9	8390.20	54	
			697.60
C_8	4185.60	48	
			348.80
C_7	2092.80	42	
			174.40
C_6	1046.40	36	
			87.20
C_5	523.20	30	
			43.60
Middle C — C_4	261.60	24	
			21.80
C_3	130.80	18	
			10.90
C_2	65.40	12	
			5.45
C_1	32.70	6	
			2.73
C_0	16.35	0	

the 8 notes of the piano, there are 6 whole steps and 2 half steps. When Pronovost makes use of the word "tones" in the above procedural steps in finding the natural pitch level, he is actually referring to whole tones, and therefore actually referring to steps within the octave.

If we look again at Table I, we see that the frequency values associated with various octaves of the note of C are accompanied by another scale setting forth tonal values for each one of these frequencies. Thus middle C, or C_4, having a frequency of 261.60 cycles per second, can also be represented as a tone lying 24 tones above C_0 or 16.35 cycles per second. We can then, by knowing what a pitch level is in tones, mathematically perform a transposition by which this pitch level can be expressed in cycles per second, or vice versa. We can do this by use of the scale shown in Table I, which divides each octave into cycles per tone. The basis behind such division is that each octave consists of 6 tones, so that the interval expressed in an octave, when divided by 6, will give the number of cycles which will be traveled in moving up the scale one tone within any given octave. For example, suppose we know that a person's median pitch level is 120 cycles per second. We immediately know that this will lie somewhere between 12 tones and 18 tones above C_0. Knowing that there are 65.40 cycles per second to be transversed within that particular octave, we can see that each tone will cover a range of approximately 11 cycles per second. Knowing also that 120 cycles per second is approximately 11 cycles below the top point of the octave, at 130.80 cycles per second, we can see that this individual's median pitch level will be approximately one tone below 18 tones above C_0. This individual's median pitch level, then, will lie at 17 tones above C_0.

Concerning the reliability of these different methods, Pronovost has stated: "In these methods the predicted natural pitch was found, on the average, to deviate from the actual median by less than one tone, while a test of reliability of these predictions on six or seven consecutive days disclosed the maximum range of deviations to be 1.5 tones. Although the results of the study afford no means of selecting the best of these five methods, other considerations appear to indicate that the 25% method is the most convenient to use."

The third term used in classifying pitch levels is the term optimum pitch level. This is the pitch level generally conceded to be best for speakers of each sex, size, age. etc. This would be the pitch which would seem to psychologically fit the individual. The concept of optimum pitch is one which is seldom used at present, since the optimum pitch level and natural pitch level usually coincide. Another term which we should make reference to at this point is the median pitch level. The median pitch level for an individual is simply the midpoint of all the pitch levels which the individual uses, and corresponds to the habitual pitch level. Pitch level will change to some degree from hour to hour, or day to day, as one is fresh or fatigued, as one is tense or relaxed, as one whispers softly to his loved one or ones or yells at his children. Generally speaking, however, most pitches which a person uses tend to fall around the habitual pitch level, or median pitch level.

The specific frequencies which are cited for median pitch level in different individuals differ depending upon the sex, degree of physical maturity, type of stimulus (factual, emotional) and mode of stimulus presented (oral reading, free speech, rote, etc.) In childhood, the median pitch level between birth and 9 months of age tends to be about 556 cps, with a range of 63 cps to 2631 cps. Expressed in tones above the zero frequency level, the median pitch level is 30.7 tones with a standard deviation of 4.6 tones. There is a general pitch level increase up to the age of 5 months when the pitch level plateaus. A gradual decrease in pitch level begins at the ninth month. Infants have much higher pitch levels than older children or adults, and also have the greatest range of pitches which can be utilized. The data from which these figures come was collected by making recordings of infants while they were crying for food (15). Somewhere between the age of 1 year and 7 years, pitch levels fall considerably for both boys and girls. Median pitch levels for both boys and girls at the age of 7 and 8 years lie around the value of 280 cps or 25 tones above the zero frequency level. The standard deviation is around 1.0 tones. The citation of standard deviation, as in the paragraph above, is probably familar to many readers. The standard deviation is a statistical description for presenting varying ability around a mean or median point.

For those who are unfamiliar with the concept of standard deviation, let us examine a few aspects of this measure: The concept of standard deviation assumes a normal distribution curve. This means simply that most of the scores, or pitch levels used, or other items considered will fall somewhere around the mean or median. Most will lie close to the mean or median, and others trail away to varying degrees. Half will fall above the median, and half below. Of the 50 per cent falling above the median, about 34 per cent will lie within the range of one standard deviation above the median, another 13 per cent in the range including two standard deviations, and the remainder in the range encompassed by three standard deviations. The same general figures will be true for the remaining half of the pitch levels found below the median. These relationships are perhaps shown more graphically in Figure 19. If we look at the standard deviation figures for 7 and 8 year old children, where both girls and boys are using essentially the

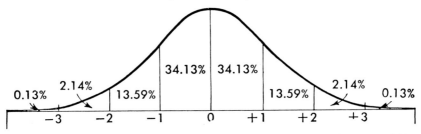

FIGURE 19. The normal distribution curve, with percentage of scores within each standard deviation specified. Note that 99.74 per cent of all scores lie between ±3 standard deviations.

same pitch levels, we note once again that the standard deviation was found to be somewhere around 1.0 tones. Since the median pitch level is 25 tones above the zero frequency level, we can say that roughly about 68 per cent of the pitch levels encountered will fall between 24 and 26 tones above 16.35 cps, about 95 per cent will fall between 23 tones and 27 tones above 16.35 cps, and essentially all of the pitch levels found will lie between 22 tones and 28 tones above the zero frequency level.

Somewhere after 8 years, children undergo that interesting age period known as puberty. During the period of puberty, voice levels fall considerably. This is particulary true with male voices.

There is an interesting anatomical reason for the decided shift in pitch level of the male voice. Somewhere during the stage of puberty, and of course this stage is encountered at different age levels by different boys, the male larynx undergoes a fundamental startling difference. The angle at which the two wings of the thyroid cartilage come together, which is the point at which the vocal folds are attached, changes. Whereas in children the two wings of the thyroid cartilage which form the apex in midline join at an angle of approximately 110 to 120 degrees, this angle during the age of puberty for males is reduced to approximately 90 degrees. This difference in the manner in which the two wings join, and the subsequent lengthening of the vocal folds which is necessitated by virtue of the fact that the vocal folds are attached to the point of junction of the wings, result in a greater mass of the vocal folds in males. The result is the production in the male of the prominence in the anterior section of the neck ordinarily termed the "Adam's apple." In women, such a change in the angle of junction of the wings of the thyroid is not noted, and consequently women have no "Adam's apple." Considerable attention has been paid to study of the pitch levels of males at varying age levels past 8 years. In general, it has been observed that the pitch levels for 10-year-old boys tend to be somewhere around 270 cycles per second, a drop of only about 20 cycles from the median pitch levels found two years earlier; the median pitch level at 14 years of age is about 240 cycles per second, a drop of another 30 cycles; and the median pitch level for 18-year-old boys has been found to be about 137 cycles per second. The upshot of all this data is the fact that somewhere between the age of 10 and 18, the usual male voice drops in pitch level by about one octave. It is also interesting to note that the standard deviation found at these different age levels tends to increase from the figure of about 1.2 tones at the age of 10 to a figure of about 1.8 tones at age 18 (16). During the period of time that the voice is shifting in the male, as he undergoes the anatomic and physiologic changes in his laryngeal structure, a phenomenon is observed which has been described as "voice breaks." Curry (17) found 20 measurable voice breaks in 10-year-old boys, 25 such breaks in 14-year-old boys, and no breaks in pitch levels of

18-year-old boys. The upward breaks (breaking from a new low pitch to the old high pitch) occurred from points lower than the median pitch by approximately one octave and had a mean extent of about 1-1/2 tones. All of the downward breaks occurred at a pitch level very close to the median pitch level and had a mean extent of about 6 tones. In general then, the voice breaks are greater in magnitude when a boy is using his old pitch level and the voice breaks down to the new pitch level than is true in the reverse situation.

In adults, median pitch levels for males tend to fall somewhere around 130 cycles per second, or C_3. This is essentially one octave below middle C. For females, median pitch levels have been reported to be somewhere around 220 cycles per second, which would be about two musical tones below middle C, or a note which corresponds to $G\sharp_3$. Further information regarding pitch levels found by different experimenters at different age levels is shown in Table II.

TABLE II

MEDIAN OR MEAN PITCH LEVEL IN CYCLES PER SECOND
COMPOSITE DATA

Age		Male	Female	Age
Infant (1-9 mo.)	(Fairbanks)	556		Infant (1-9 mo.)
7	(Fairbanks)	294	281	7 (Fairbanks)
8	(Fairbanks)	297	288	8 (Fairbanks)
10	(Curry)	269.7	258	11 (Duffy)
14	(Curry)	241.5	252 (premenstrual)	13 (Duffy)
			238 (post-menstrual)	13 (Duffy)
18	(Curry)	137.1	230	15 (Duffy)
College Age (Superior Speakers)	(Snidecor)	129		
Adult	(Hanley)	118.6	199.8	Adult (Linke)
	(Pronovost)	132.1	212	(Snidecor)
	(Cowan)	141	233	(Cowan)
	(Snidecor)	120		
Middle Age (47.9 years)	(Mysak)	110.3		
Elder Group I (73.3 years)	(Mysak)	124.9	196.6 (72.6 years)	(McGlone &
Elder Group II (85.0 years)	(Mysak)	142.6	199.8 (85.0 years)	Hollien)

Variations in median pitch level because of sex, degree of physical maturity, type of material, as well as emotional state of the individual, have already been discussed. Two other situations can serve to alter figures obtained for median pitch levels. Murray and Tiffin (18) studied poor and good voices from a beginning speech class and compared these voices to those of trained speech instructors. A tendency was shown for the poor voices to show greater extremes in the ranges of median pitch level. Snidecor (19) compared pitch levels obtained in oral reading and impromptu speaking and found slightly higher pitch levels for males during impromptu speaking than in reading.

We now turn our attention to the concept of pitch range. Pitch range refers to the total extent of pitches from the highest frequency which the vocal mechanism produces to the lowest frequency over a given period of time. This is usually quoted in a number of musical tones covered. In lay terminology it is often reported in octaves or fractions thereof. It may also be referred to in percentages, with the total pitch range being 100 per cent. Another term which has been used in discussing pitch range is that of the median 90 per cent pitch range. This is also referred to as the functional pitch range. Again this is a difference in musical units or cycles per second between high and low tones, but with statistical manipulation performed which excludes the highest and lowest 5 per cent of the pitches. Five per cent is lost at each end of the range. Within this more restricted range are located most of the frequencies used in speaking. Beyond this range, in the last 5 per cent at each end of the range, are frequencies which are not normally used in oral communication even though it is functionally possible to produce them.

Generally speaking, we are born with a tremendously wide pitch range, as we enter school our pitch range narrows considerably, and by the time we are adults we learn to expand it to some degree once again. Infants, when hungry, have a total pitch range of about 5-1/2 octaves, and a median 90 per cent pitch range of about 2-1/2 octaves (20). Seven- and eight-year-old children have a total range of about 1-1/2 octaves, and a 90 per cent range of about 1/2 an octave (21). Older boys have been reported to have a total range of about 1 and 2/3 octaves,

and a functional pitch range of about 1 octave. Both the total
range and 90 per cent range of the infant is quite great compared
to later childhood. There is a decrement beginning to become
apparent at the end of the first year. In adulthood, both males
and females have been reported to have a total pitch range of
about 1 and 2/3 octaves and a functional pitch range of about 1
octave. Snidecor (22) has stated there was a great extent of
overlap in the total range of pitches used by both sexes. Approximately 50 per cent of the pitches used by women fell below the
highest pitch used by men. Trained readers have a greater pitch
range and standard deviation than is true for untrained readers
(23). It is interesting to note that for most adults, the pitch range
is over an octave, and even the functional pitch range approxi-
mates that figure. This would indicate that for most of us, there
is available a considerable extent of pitch range which can be
used to avoid monotony in the voice.

It is also possible to change pitch during the act of speaking.
There are two general kinds of pitch change which have been
reported. The first of these is termed a pitch shift (also referred
to as a step, or a skip). This is a term applied to a change in
pitch level, up or down, between phonations. It is a shift which
occurs during the time when we are catching our breath to begin
talking again. Shifts occur within and between phrases with shifts
between phrases usually being of greater extent. Upward shifts
apparently exceed downward shifts in both amount of shift and frequency of occurrence (24). The second kind of pitch change is
termed an inflection. This is a pitch change without interruption
of phonation. Change in pitch level may be up and down, up or
down, or any combination of these. Inflections involving one or
more changes of direction within any phonation are called cir-
cumflex. Downward inflections ordinarily exceed upward inflections in both extent and number. Snidecor (25) states that downward inflections are more numerous than upward inflections but
are not markedly different in mean extent. Fairbanks and Pronovost (26) in studying emotionally charged passages reported that
downward inflections were wider and greater in number than
upward inflections in simulation of all emotions studied. Within
phrases, inflections were found to be wider than shifts, and to

outnumber shifts four to one. Tiffin and Steer (27) found wider inflections on stressed words than on the same words in unstressed positions in 84 per cent of the observations made.

Philhour (28) in a doctoral dissertation found no significant relationship between either range or extent of inflection or any other physical measure of variability with general excellence or pitch excellence of a voice.

Many experimenters have reported upon the rate of pitch change for inflection in terms of the number of tones per second utilized in the inflection. In general, it appears that the rate of change increases with age, particularly so in the case of the male, who consistently uses more changes than the female. Emotion (insofar as simulated emotion can be accepted as being representative) tends to produce a greater rate of change. Reading produces a greater rate of change than impromptu speaking. Using one's habitual pitch or a pitch slightly above this produces a greater rate of change than does a pitch lower than the habitual one. Attempting to increase the flexibility of one's production does not noticeably change the rate, whereas decreasing the flexibility considerably slows the rate of pitch change.

All the foregoing, including the description of pitch level, total pitch range, median 90 per cent range, types of pitch change, extent of pitch change and rate of pitch change when viewed compositely are grouped under the term "pitch variability." There are some general statements which can be made regarding pitch variability. Pitch variability tends to increase with age, males have greater pitch variability than females, emotional or dramatic material produces greater pitch variability than does factual material, trained voices exhibit greater pitch variability than untrained, habitual use of the natural pitch level or slightly above this produces greater variability than does a lower pitch, and oral reading of material produces greater pitch variability than impromptu speaking.

Let us now turn our attention to problems that may show up in the realm of pitch. First of all, a pitch can be too high. An habitual pitch may be well above what the natural pitch would prescribe. Secondly, a pitch can be too low. An habitual pitch may be well below the natural pitch. There can also be a lack of flexibility or variety in pitch, giving a very monotonous effect to one's speaking. And finally, pitch patterns can be established. Pitch patterns can be established by inflexibility in rate, continual use of a rising or falling inflectional pattern, continual over-inflection, or continual under-inflection. These are all matters which demand attention in terms of seeking to improve the speaking voice. Generally speaking, a person can work by himself to improve matters of pitch range. That is, he can develop greater flexibility or variety in pitch, can develop the use of a greater shift and inflection pattern in his speech, and work to avoid any monotonous effect which may be transmitted by his use of inflection. Sometimes he may need some guidance. However, in terms of pitch level, if a person's voice is too high or too low, there is a need for professional attention. Such attention will probably be forthcoming with the combined efforts of a laryngologist, who will examine the vocal structures and see whether there is a physiological reason why pitch may be too high or too low, and a speech pathologist, who can work with the individual in order to modify the noted deviation in pitch. There is a danger for persons who, when feeling that their pitch is too high or too low, set out to work upon the problem themselves. All too often, by so doing, the ground work is laid for future serious organic problems. Remember that pitch level is a function of balances between the length, tension and mass of the vocal folds. In a vocal mechanism such balances or adjustments are arrived at over a span of many years. The average pitch level of an individual has changed considerably from his childhood to the time when he is a young adult. Working on one's own to produce some kind of great change in that balance can result in much vocal strain and perhaps even more serious defects (29).

There are a number of reasons in addition to vocal strain why pitch problems might occur. A person could have faulty pitch discrimination. This could be related to some kind of organic problem or it could be functional. He may also have poor tonal memory. This again could be functional or it could be delimited by the mental capacity of the individual. There can be poor motor control, as in many central nervous system disorders. There might be an emotional maladjustment. This would most often have its effect on pitch during the pubescent stage. The manifestation insofar as pitch is concerned would be shown in pubescent vocalizations. Faulty learning in general can cause pitch deviations. There may not be a problem with faulty learning, but simply a lack of learning. Pitch deviations may produce changes in vocal quality. Voice quality problems can be determined if they are heard independently of specific phonemes. In other words, voice quality problems will occur not on only one or two phonemes, but on most phonemes. A pitch level lower than the natural pitch often leads to breathy quality. Such quality results when the vocal folds fail to approximate completely as they vibrate and a steady stream of air rushes audibly through the glottis and resonance cavities. There is apparently an optimum condition of vocal fold tension in relation to a given amount of breath pressure below the vocal folds. Often when there is too much tension in a strain to produce adequate loudness at low pitches, a harshness can result. This harsh quality is characterized by noisy, raspy, unmusical tones. When particularly low pitched, such harshness is often called guttural; and when particularly high pitched, such harshness is often called strident. Sometimes attempts to produce adequate volume at lower tones or a simple attempt to produce lower tones will result in hoarseness. This quality is typical of the individual who has acute or chronic laryngitis. More information regarding vocal quality problems will be discussed in the section on Voice Quality.

We have mentioned earlier that other factors in addition to the simple rate of vibration of the vocal folds can lead to perception of pitch level in the individual. One of the most important of these secondary factors is that of intensity. This is a phenomenon which occurs at the vocal fold level. Holding intensity constant, a high fundamental frequency of vibration is associated with a greater energy concentration in the lower overtones. This effect is found up to a fundamental frequency of about 250 cycles per second. If one uses a fundamental frequency higher than this, greater energy is found in the higher overtones of the vocal fold fundamental frequency. Holding frequency constant, that is, using the same habitual pitch level, increasing intensity generally produces more energy concentration in the high overtones of the fundamental frequency produced by the vocal folds (30). This information is of some value in speech therapy, since one method by which pitch level can be changed is by changing the intensity level of the voice. If a voice sounds too low, increasing intensity without changing pitch level will generally produce a pitch level which sounds somewhat higher.

PART TWO

TIME, INTENSITY AND QUALITY

IV

TIME AND DURATION IN SPEECH

I T IS IMPORTANT TO REALIZE that all speech is actually a series
of "noises" or "phonations" and "silences" or "pauses." Duration
is the length of time involved in the production of a single sound.
As we look for information regarding the duration of phonations
and pauses, we see that experimentation in this area began as
early as 1934. At that time, Murray and Tiffin (31) stated that
the mean duration of phonation for a given sound in seconds is
about 1/10 of a second. Three groups of speakers were used in
establishing this result—poor, good and trained speakers. It was
also observed that the trained speakers had more flexibility in the
duration of their phonations than poor speakers did. Wang (32)
found that 57 of 66 vowel attempts lasted approximately .12
seconds, with 5 vowels before voiceless consonants lasting about
.1 second and 4 vowels at .14 second occurring before voiced consonants. Parmenter and Trevino (33) obtained results from a subject from the Middle West who read narrative prose and secured
information regarding the absolute and relative length of different
speech sounds. This particular Mid-westerner spent 76 per cent of
the total time reading the passage in phonation. Of this 76 per
cent, 36 per cent was occupied by vowels (or about 45 per cent
of the entire time spent in reading). The remainder of the time
was filled in the following manner: voiced consonants, 40 per cent;
voiceless consonants and pauses. 24 per cent; all consonants and
pauses (everything, that is, except vowels), 55 per cent. Roughly
speaking, there were almost twice as many consonants as vowels
in the passage, but the time occupied by the two did not differ
greatly. This would indicate that each vowel lasted on the average
about twice as long as each consonant. Once more the average
duration of phonation was around 1/10 of a second. The length
of stressed vowels was almost 75 per cent greater than the dura-

tion of unstressed vowels. This information is shown in Table III.
In general, then, stressed vowels have a greater duration than un

TABLE III

VOWEL DURATION

	% of Total Vowels	% of Total Time in Seconds	Average Time
Stressed	44%	57%	.15 sec.
Unstressed	56%	43%	.08 sec.

(From Parmenter and Trevino, p. 131.)

stressed vowels, and any kind of vowel has a longer duration than
any kind of consonant. Table IV reports the particular phonemes
which were observed to possess the longest and shortest durations.

Mysak (34) reported that age seems to have an effect upon the
percentage of total speaking time devoted to phonations. Middle-
aged males spent 56 per cent of the total time in phonations,
whereas in elderly males phonations occupied about 50 per cent

TABLE IV

THE SIX LONGEST AND SHORTEST SOUNDS (DURATION)

Longest	Shortest
[aɪ]—.191 sec.	[ŋ]—.047 sec.
[ɛɪ]—.188	[t]—.060
[æ]—.152	[l]—.060
[oʊ]—.151	[h]—.061
[i]—.138	[ð]—.061
[a]—.127	[v]—.063

(From Parmenter and Trevino, p. 132.)

of the total time. Snidecor (35) earlier had reported phonations
occupying 65 per cent of total time.

It is interesting to note that durations of syllables can produce
differences in words perceived by listeners. An experiment was
performed at the Bell Telephone Laboratories (36) in which
speech was produced artificially, the process known as synthetic
speech. More regarding such work will be contained in the chapter
on Voice Quality. A two-syllable word, such as the word "object"

was synthesized. Several samples were made of each one of the test words utilized. The frequencies contained in all the samples were identical. This means that on the basis of the frequency information contained, all samples of each word were identical. The durations of the syllables, however, were different in each of the test words. In some samples, the vowel in the first syllable was made longer in duration than the vowel in the second syllable; in other samples, the duration of the second vowel was made longer than that of the vowel in the first syllable. The words with the longer vowel in the first syllable were heard with the stress on the first syllable, as in "the *ob*ject." When the vowel of the second syllable was made longer, listeners heard the stress on the second syllable, and regarded the word as "to ob*ject.*" This experiment reveals that the duration, rather than the intensity, of the vowels can determine the stress perceived by the listener. Shifting stress from one syllable to another had another effect. If you listen to someone say the words "the *ob*ject" and "to ob*ject,*" you note that the vowel in the first syllable is pronounced differently in the two words. Listeners perceived the same effect as they listened to these samples of words produced synthetically. When the second syllable was longer, listeners perceived an unstressed vowel in the first syllable. When the first syllable was long, however, listeners perceived an [a] vowel appropriate to the stressed syllable. Listeners identified two separate sounds having exactly the same frequency information as being different vowels, depending upon their duration.

Let us now turn our attention to the duration of pauses. Murray and Tiffin (37) found a mean duration in seconds for pauses ranging from .80 to 1.4, with .80 being most frequent. This would indicate that the average length of a pause was around .8 of a second. Parmenter and Trevino (38), as indicated before, found the total percentage of time not occupied by phonation as being 24 per cent. Percentages of 44 to 50 were reported by Mysak (39) and 35 per cent by Snidecor (40). Fewer than one-third of the pauses recorded by Parmenter and Trevino occurred between sentences, the rest occurred within sentences. However, the average duration of the pauses between the sentences was about four times as long as the duration of pauses within sentences.

Table V reveals some information from a study by Darley (41) regarding oral reading rate for three types of material read by college freshmen. The average reading rate with average material was 167 words or 440 syllables per minute. Franke (42) attempted to determine what rates were considered too fast and too slow. College students were used as judges. Graduate students read stan-

TABLE V

MEDIAN RATE OF SPEECH

Passage	Words per Min.	Syllables per Min.
1. "Average" material	167	440
2. Polysyllabic	115	660
3. Monosyllabic	201	300

(From Darley.)

dard passages aloud. These college students judged a rate somewhere between 140 and 185 words per minute as being acceptable. The mean rate was 157 words per minute. Kelly and Steer (43) sought the same kind of information for extemporaneous speaking performances. The mean rate was found to be 159 words per minute. Interestingly, they found a range of more than 200 words per minute from the average slowest sentence to the average fastest sentence in the samples of extemporaneous speech which they analyzed. It is known that rate decreases in difficult speaking circumstances, such as in the presence of high level noise. Abrams *et al.* (44) found a mean rate of 140 words per minute when speakers were exposed to high noise levels. Interestingly, college students serving as judges thought that the optimum rate would be closer to 100 words per minute in this noise situation. Draegert (45) found that the factor of syllable duration was a statistically significant means of differentiating between best and worst communicators when communication took place in high noise levels.

Rate is influenced by the number of pauses and phonations. There are two approaches which may be taken to alter a too rapid rate: (a) a speaker may take longer pauses while he is talking, and (b) he may lengthen the phonations, ordinarily during the vowels. On the other hand, a slow rate of speech can be made more rapid by shortening both the pauses and the phonations.

General temperamental and personality characteristics influence a person's speech. If his motor activities are done with rapidity, speech will tend to be rapid. If the person, on the other hand, is usually slow in everything he does, his speech rate will be slow also. In addition, the speaker's attitude toward what he is saying and his purpose with regard to his listeners will influence his rate. Such states as wonder, doubt, confusion, reverence, sorrow and deep thought are more conducive to a slow tempo; whereas states such as joy, excitement, anger, humor and a feeling of confidence and well-being are more closely connected to a rapid rate.

Phrasing refers to the act of dividing words spoken or read into groups, by the device of introducing into the time sequence pauses long enough in duration to perform this function. A phrase, then, is a continuance of utterance bounded by pauses. Such use of the word implies that any given series of words may be divided up in a number of different ways. Phrases in speaking may not coincide whatsoever with grammatical phrases, clauses, or sentences. When listeners are asked to judge words included within a spoken phrase, they seem to be guided to some degree by the duration of the pauses at the limits of the phrase. Snidecor (46) found that as the mean duration of the pauses at the phrase limits became longer, more listeners agreed upon the exact number of words included within the phrase. Remember that the student of grammar divides a sentence into parts, following rules of structure which are definite. A speaker, however, can be considerably more arbitrary, since his only objective is to assist the listener to get a better understanding of his meaning. His phrasing in large part is determined by his judgment. Consequently, many different individuals would break up thought groups into phrases in many different fashions. Phrases identified as such by 50 per cent or more of listeners are reliably longer than those which are identified by fewer than 50 per cent of the listeners (47). More words are ordinarily used per phrase in a reading situation than in an impromptu speaking situation.

There are certain identifiable relationships between phrases and pitch phenomena. For example, pitch movements throughout phrases tend to be downward, particularly in reading. If a speaker makes a statement, he generally uses a downward inflection toward the end of the last phrase. If he asks a question, on the other hand, he usually uses an upward inflection toward the end of the last phrase. There are also some consistencies in the variation of duration of pauses between phrases. Generally a long pause after a phrase indicates relative finality. A short pause indicates incompleteness of the idea. If the phrase preceding a long pause ends with a downward inflection, the effect of finality mentioned is obtained, and the emphasis is turned back, as it were, upon the preceding phrase. On the other hand, if an upward inflection has been used, the long pause tends to emphasize the following phrase by holding it after the rising inflection has caused it to be anticipated.

Rhythm is usually thought of as being primarily an element of form, such as the relationship between stressed and unstressed syllables. It is created by a regular recurrence of any such relationship. In the psychological sense, it means the perception of a series of stimuli as a series of groups of stimuli. The successive groups are ordinarily of similar pattern and described as being repetitive. Rhythm includes a combination of attack and release of sound, rise and fall of inflection, and pattern of phonation and pause. There are at least three different factors which influence rhythm: One of these is simply the thought which the speaker is trying to communicate. Remember that prose as well as poetry should be read to express meaning, and not primarily to expose the rhythmical pattern. The temperament of an individual in a given situation will influence rhythm. For example, anger generally would elicit a faster rhythmical pattern, whereas sorrow would elicit a slower pattern; and finally the type of language used will produce great change in the rhythmic patterns observed. For example, the pentameter of Shakespeare compared with lines of blank verse illustrate how different types of language lend themselves to different rhythmic patterns. In general, too much rhythm becomes monotonous, and too little rhythm is described as "jerky." In some speech problems, particularly those of stuttering or cluttering, the flow of speech and the rhythm thereof are broken by hesitations, or stoppages, or repetitions, or prolongations of particular sounds. At one time, both stuttering and cluttering were classified as disorders of rhythm, and some textbooks will still refer to them by this name.

V

INTENSITY AND LOUDNESS

INTENSITY, A PHYSICAL MEASUREMENT, refers to the force with which energy is given off by the sound source, or the energy with which a sound wave strikes an object, such as the eardrum. The amount of energy thus produced is dependent upon the amplitude. In considering the sound wave, the amount of energy being transmitted along the wave, per square centimeter of wave front, is called intensity. This shows that intensity has to do with the flow of energy in the wave of compression.

The acoustic energy of normal speech is very, very, small. Our vocal folds can convert only a portion of the energy of the air stream flowing from our lungs into acoustic energy, actually only about 1/20 of 1 per cent. The energy of a speech wave during 1 second of speech is only about 200 ergs. It would take about a billion ergs to keep a 100 watt light bulb lit for one second.

When we are 6 feet from a buzzing fly, the ear collects only a small fraction of the sound which the fly produces. The sphere of sound produced by the fly is about 12 feet in diameter. The surface of this sphere would have an area of about 65,000 square inches. Consequently, when we are 6 feet away the sound we hear is about 1/300,000 fly power. It is actually much less than this, for not all the fly's power is used in producing sound (48).

Keep in mind that to some degree sound always dissipates and disappears as it travels. Its energy is lost in heating the air through which it moves. Sounds of higher pitch are used up more quickly than lower-pitched sounds, but in hundreds of miles virtually all the sound will have turned into heat.

The expression of intensity of a sound is given as a ratio rather than an absolute magnitude. The intensity of a sound at a point is often expressed in terms of the amplitude of the pressure or power of the sound, but is much more often expressed as decibels, which are ratios. The propagation of a sound wave in air depends upon rapid alternation of air particle displacement, and is associated with changes in pressure, velocity, temperature and air density. Methods of measuring intensity of sounds are therefore based on determination of one or more of these fundamental phenomena.

In considering the measurement of intensity the following concept must be kept clear: The range of vibration (degree of amplitude) of the sound source will determine the intensity (or amplitude) of the sound wave.

Intensity may be measured by at least three different methods: (a) as the alternating pressure of the sound wave; (b) as the velocity with which air particles move to and fro, and (c) as a flow of energy in horsepower or watts. When sound emanates from a vibrating object, it is proper to speak in terms of the power of that sound. That power is released in all directions. When we try to measure the power, however, we generally do so in terms of pressure units. We do so because of the fact that when a force, or power, strikes some object standing in the path of that force, it is no longer proper to speak of power of the sound. Power, when striking an object standing in the path of the sound, is converted to pressure. Whenever we place a microphone in the path of a sound to measure it, we obtain readings that deal with pressure units. The unit ordinarily used in measuring pressure directly is entitled dynes per square centimeter. In resistive media (such as air) power is always proportional to the square of the pressure. Pressure is ordinarily used as a measurement of force of a sound because most recording instruments are responsive to the alternating pressure variations. Pressure is a measure of power per unit of area. The energy present is ordinarily measured as an average rate of a flow of energy through some unit of area. The amount of energy, as discussed earlier, is actually very small. It has been estimated that it would take 4 million people, all talking at once at an ordinary conversational level, to produce enough energy to light a single ordinary 40 watt light bulb. In normal conversational speech, when a listener stands some 3 feet from the speaker, the average sound pressure received is about halfway along the total intensity scale to which the human ear can respond. The sound which the listener receives is about 1 million times stronger than the weakest audible sound and about 1 million times weaker than the strongest sound we can hear without feeling pain. This intensity would measure about 65 dB greater than 10^{-16} watts per square centimeter, which is the intensity of a just barely audible sound. This intensity would correspond to a pressure variation of about $\frac{1}{1,000,000}$ of normal atmospheric pressure. The varying sound pressures found in speech are, then, only a very small fraction of the air pressure that always surrounds us. In other words, speech is composed of weak, weaker and extreme weakest sounds. When such measurements are taken, revealing that the intensity level of normal conversational speech is somewhere around 65 dB greater than 10^{-16} watts per square centimeter, this figure itself is an average of the pressure or intensity values of speech over several seconds of time. The intensity of speech actually varies considerably about this average value. Even if we ask someone to speak steadily at some normal conversation level, the speech intensities vary greatly as he pronounces one speech sound after another. As we shall see later, the intensity of different phonemes varies over a range of about 680 to 1.

To consider the relation between intensity and distance, one must first understand that sound energy is transmitted equally in all directions from its source. The basic rule is "sound varies inversely as the square of the distance from the source." This is called the "Inverse Square Law." A sound of given intensity at a given distance (say 6 feet) has 1/4 that intensity at twice the distance (12 feet), and 1/9 the intensity at 3 times the distance (18 feet). Since intensity in a homogenous atmosphere falls off inversely as the square of the distance from the source, sounds of higher frequency will be first to fall below the intensity necessary for minimum audibility, and will cease to be heard while sounds of lower frequency can still be detected. Lower frequencies are always more intense in speech.

Let us turn our attention to the discussion of the term loudness. Loudness is a psychological function of intensity; the term refers to the strength of the sensation received through the ear. When a sound of any character is impressed upon the ear, the magnitude of the sensation produced is called the loudness. Two sounds which are of equal intensity may not necessarily be regarded as equally loud. The loudness of a sound is related to the work done in producing it, and so we can see why to speak loudly requires more effort than to speak quietly. Loudness is a sensation, a psychological concept, which is related to the magnitude of the sound, but does not mean the same thing. Persons active in the field of Voice Science have spent years on the determination of scales to relate intensity and loudness. A scale of equal loudness has been constructed, the units of which are called phons. The reference point, or the basis for the Phon Scale, is the loudness of a 1000 cycle per second tone at 40 decibels. This amount of loudness is called 40 phons. Another suggestion to relate intensity and loudness is to create a scale in which the basic unit of loudness is concurrent with the least perceptible increment of intensity. The problem with this scheme is that equal intensity numbers or scales do not correspond to tones sounding equally loud. For example, a tone of 128

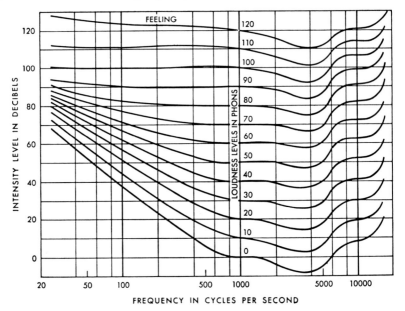

FIGURE 20. Loudness level contours vs. intensity levels. Curves are labeled with loudness level measured in phons. (Reprinted with permission from Denes and Pinson, *The Speech Chain,* 1963, Bell Telephone Laboratories.)

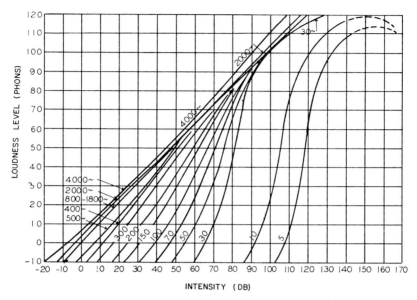

FIGURE 21. Loudness Level as a function of Intensity Level. Since the Loudness Level for 1000 cps is defined as the Intensity Level of that tone, the curve for 1000 cps (800-1800 cps in the figure) appears as a straight line with a slope of 1. (Reprinted with permission from Stevens and Davis, *Hearing: Its Psychology and Physiology,* 1938, John Wiley & Sons, Inc.)

cycles per second with a sensation level of 40 decibels sounds equally loud to a tone of 16 cps with a sensation level of 70 decibels. On the Phon Scale, both of these points would have a loudness level of about 10 phons.

Loudness is not synonomous with intensity. Intensity is a physical element of sound and can be observed with the aid of instruments. Loudness, like pitch, cannot be measured directly. It is measured only through the interpretation of persons listening to stimuli. The stimuli can be measured. The intensity of a sound increases at a much greater rapidity than does its loudness. At 1000 cycles per second the ear can distinguish about 400 degrees of loudness between 0 decibels and 130 decibels.

Another term often used to describe some characteristic of power or pressure of a sound is volume. Volume is a word used to describe the manner in which sounds seem to fill space. This is another psychological concept, somewhat similar to loudness, but more inclusive. Volume seems to be correlated with the following: (a) Frequency. With intensity held constant, the lower the frequency the greater the volume. (b) Intensity. With frequency held constant, the greater the intensity the greater the volume. (c) Wave composition. With both frequency and intensity held constant, the more components to a complex wave the greater the volume. While loudness varies with both amplitude and frequency, volume apparently varies positively with amplitude, but negatively with frequency. No reliable measurements of volume have been made, and this term is seldom used at this time as a precise indication of any particular factor of the sound wave.

In comparing the intensities of two sounds, the ratio of the energy flow per second is compared. The logarithm of the two energies producing the ratio is ordinarily used; this is termed a bel, in honor of Alexander Graham Bell. A bel may be defined as the logarithm of the ratio between two intensities. When we are dealing with logarithms, the change from one number to another, as in the difference from 5 bels to 6 bels, is a tremendous jump in actual physical stimulus. If we look at Table VI, we can see the tremendous change introduced from moving from 5 bels to 6 bels. We can also note in Table VI the tremendous range of power or pressure variations to which the ear can respond. In terms of the actual power of sounds, the ear can respond to a range of approximately 100,000,000,000,000. Throughout this entire range the human ear can make useful discriminations and comparisons concerning differential intensity of sounds.

With such a tremendous range in which to work, our senses must have some particular ways of dealing with sound powers. In 1834 the German physicist E.H. Weber laid down a fundamental principle: that a stimulus must be increased by a constant fraction of its value to be just noticeably different. For an example of how the Weber principle operated, let us take two pencils. If we lay the pencils down before us, we can see whether one pencil is any longer than the other. With such a comparison, we can expect that the difference that will be just noticeable to our eye would be some portion of an inch: perhaps 1/16 inch, or 1/8 inch, when the pencils are held close to us. However, if we place the pencils across the room, and look at them from a distance of 20 feet, we can expect that it would be difficult to notice a difference of 1/8 inch. One pencil might have to be 10 per cent longer than the other for us to notice a difference. Perhaps the difference might be closer to 5 per cent, or perhaps 20 per cent. If the just noticeable difference is somewhere around 10 per cent, then one pencil might have to be 5 1/2 inches long if the other is 5 inches long. One pencil might have to be 11 inches long if the other is 10 inches long. Weber's principle states that it is this percentage difference that is important in distinguishing the magnitudes of stimuli such as sounds (50). Experiments show that the least distinguishable difference in intensity of a sound is much more often a fraction of the sound's power than it is to some constant difference in power. Weber's principle is at least approximately true. Since this is the case, it has made greater sense to formulate a system in which sounds are measured on the basis of the ratio of their powers than on the strict difference of their powers.

Another German physicist, Gustav Fechner, in 1860, published a work entitled *Elemente Der Psychophysik* (Elements of Psychophysics). Fechner went one step further than Weber had, asserting that a sensory response to a stimulus increases by a constant amount whenever the stimulus is increased by a constant factor. In other words, each time we double the intensity or power of a sound, we also increase the sensation of loudness of that sound by a constant amount. The Fechner principle also emphasizes the importance of ratios rather than absolute differences in sound powers. It has been proven experimentally that Fechner's principle does not actually work over the entire range of powers of sound to which the human ear can attend. Actually, if we increase the sound power or the intensity by about 8 times, we double the sensation of loudness. Fechner's principle would suggest that rather than doubling the sensation of loudness, the sensation of loudness would be increased by a given amount. Nevertheless, it is possible to see the importance of calculating sound power in terms of ratios. In general, persons do judge the relative loudness of sounds in terms of ratios of powers rather than in terms of actual differences in powers. We judge one sound to be louder than another, or twice as loud as another, or softer than another, etc.

Recall that the logarithm of the ratio between two intensities was defined as a bel. The human ear can distinquish and tolerate sound within a range of 13 to 14 bels, and therefore the bel is too large a unit for precise accurate measurement. The bel has therefore been divided by 10, and each new step is called a decibel (1/10 of a bel). Since the human ear can distinguish 13 to 14 bels, and each bel make 10 decibels, there are 130 to 140 decibels in the average human hearing range, from the weakest sound which can be detected to the most powerful sound which can be tolerated. The bels count the number of steps a decimal point comes to the right of a chain of zeroes (since the bel is a logarithm, 1 bel means 10 times the power, 2 bels means 100 times the power, 3 bels means 1000 times the power, and so on). One log unit to the base 10 of the ratio of one acoustic power to another is one bel.

Logarithmic scales are used in all measurements which have to do with the physical senses, particularly those of vision and hearing. On such a scale, we are dealing with the exponents (10^2, 10^3, 10^4) of some constant number, called the base. In the case of the logarithms we are mentioning now, the base is the number 10. We must keep in mind that whenever we see a number with an exponent, it stands for a larger number. For example, 10^3 means the same thing as 1000. Such a logarithmic scale has only one notable drawback; it lacks a zero point. Therefore it is a scale of ratios, always comparing two different things. One must be sure to realize what the quantity is with which another quantity in sound measurement is being compared. When we are interested only in the relationship between two intensities, one of them becomes the reference for the other. When we wish to represent absolute values, however, it is necessary first to pick some reference level, call this the zero point, and compare all other intensities with this zero reference point. The standard reference point in acoustical measurement is a sound pressure of .0002 dynes per square centimeter. This particular reference point was chosen because of the fact that this amount of pressure acting upon the ear drum will bring about a reaction of hearing from the individual. A dyne is a very small unit of pressure. To support a 1 ounce weight against the force of gravity, for example, we have to exert an upward force of about 28,000 dynes. The pressure acting on the ear drum at the very threshold of hearing then is around 140 million times smaller in pressure than is needed to lift a 1 ounce weight. Since the usual way to measure speech sounds is not by power, but by sound pressure, the following formula is used:

$$N \text{ (number of decibels)} = 20 \log_{10} Pr_1 / \!\! / Pr_0$$

$$Pr_0 = 0.0002 \text{ dynes per square centimeter}$$

Pr_1 is the sound pressure in question, and Pr_0 is the reference level, .0002 dynes per square centimeter. This is the reference point used in practically all acoustical measurement, and will be the reference point referred to in figures in subsequent sections of this book.

One must always keep in mind that the decibel is not an absolute unit of measurement like an inch. It is a relative unit. It tells by what proportion one value is greater than another. One cannot say that the intensity of a given sound is fifty decibels. It must be fifty decibels above or below some other sound having some other value of intensity. For example, if sound A has ten times the power of sound B, it is 10 decibels greater than sound B. If sound C has one hundred times the sound pressure of sound B, it is 40 decibels greater.

1. 1 dB = a power increase of 26%. If one sound is 1 dB greater than another, the ratio of the first will be 1.26 (126%) that of the second.
   In other words, P_2 = 1.259 (1.26) greater than P_1 (P = power)

$$\frac{P_2}{P_1} = \frac{1.26}{1}$$

2. Doubling the power = 3 db increase
3. 3.16 x the power = 5 db increase
4. Keep shifting the number of times the base number is multiplied by itself as you progress:

$$\underline{\text{Power}}$$

$$\frac{1.00}{1.00} = \frac{1}{1} = 0 \ \text{dB}$$

$$\frac{1.26}{1.00} = \frac{1.26}{1} = 1 \ \text{dB}$$

$$\frac{(1.26)(1.26)}{1.00} = \frac{1.59}{1} = 2 \ \text{dB}$$

$$\frac{(1.26) \ (1.26) \ (1.26)}{1.00} = \frac{2.0}{1} = 3 \ \text{dB}$$

$$\frac{(1.26) \ (1.26) \ (1.26) \ (1.26)}{1.000} = \frac{2.52}{1} = 4 \ \text{dB}$$

$$\frac{(1.26) \ (1.26) \ (1.26) \ (1.26) \ (1.26)}{1.00} = \frac{3.17}{1} = 5 \ \text{dB}$$

The same idea of establishing relationships between power and decibels can also be performed for pressure relationships and decibels. For any decibel value, the amount of relative sound pressure will be the square root of the amount of relative power. For this reason, each decibel shows an increase in sound pressure of 12 per cent, or a ratio of 1.12 over the pressure of another sound. The following table then can be transcribed:

$$\underline{\text{Pressure}}$$

$$\frac{1.00}{1.00} = \frac{1}{1} = 0 \ \text{db}$$

$$\frac{1.12}{1.00} = \frac{1.12}{1} = 1 \ \text{db}$$

$$\frac{(1.12) \ (1.12)}{1.00} = \frac{1.26}{1} = 2 \ \text{db}$$

$$\frac{(1.12) \ (1.12) \ (1.12)}{1.00} = \frac{1.41}{1} = 3 \ \text{db}$$

Table VI incorporates the information found in the last few pages, and is a chart showing a relationship between decibels, bels, power ratio, pressure ratio and power expressed in watts. This should be a relatively handy table of assistance to the student, and is something to which a student might sometimes wish to refer. It will be noted that once the table reaches a value of 10 decibels, succeeding jumps are only in 10 decibel intervals. Unfortunately, however, sometimes sounds may relate to one

TABLE VI

DECIBELS AND BELS: POWER-PRESSURE CHART

Pressure Ratio	Power Ratio	dB	Bels	Watts/cm²
10,000,000/1	100,000,000,000,C00/1	140	14	10^{-2}
3162277.66/1	10,000,000,000,C00/1	130	13	10^{-3}
1,000,000/1	1,000,000,000,000/1	120	12	10^{-4}
316227.77/1	100,000,000,000/1	110	11	10^{-5}
100,000/1	10,000,000,000/1	100	10	10^{-6}
31,622.78/1	1,000,000,000/1	90	9	10^{-7}
10,000/1	100,000,000/1	80	8	10^{-8}
3,162.28/1	10,000,000/1	70	7	10^{-9}
1,000/1	1,000,000/1	60	6	10^{-10}
316.23/1	100,000/1	50	5	10^{-11}
100/1	10,000/1	40	4	10^{-12}
31.62/1	1,000/1	30	3	10^{-13}
10/1	100/1	20	2	10^{-14}
3.16/1	10/1	10	1	10^{-15}
2.81/1	8.01/1	9	.9	$10^{-15.11}$
2.51/1	6.35/1	8	.8	$10^{-15.22}$
2.24/1	5.04/1	7	.7	$10^{-15.33}$
2.00/1	4.00/1	6	.6	$10^{-15.44}$
1.78/1	3.17/1	5	.5	$10^{-15.55}$
1.59/1	2.52/1	4	.4	$10^{-15.66}$
1.41/1	2.00/1	3	.3	$10^{-15.77}$
1.26/1	1.59/1	2	.2	$10^{-15.88}$
1.12/1	1.26/1	1	.1	$10^{-15.99}$

another in other than 10 decibel jumps. When this is the case, one must keep in mind that the decibel scale is a logarithmic scale. When dealing with a logarithmic scale, interpositions are established by multiplication or division of the units represented. For example, if we wish to find the power differential represented by a difference in two sounds of 23 decibels, we approach the problem in the following manner: First, regard the 23 decibels as being composed of 20 decibels plus an additional 3 decibels. Second, find the power relationships for 20 decibels and for 3 decibels. The power relationship for 20 decibels is 100, and for 3 decibels is 2. Third, *multiply* these power relationships together, or in other words, in this particular example, multiply the 100 times the 2. The total power relationship, then, expressed in a difference of 23 decibels is 200. One sound which is 23 decibels greater than another is 200 times more powerful than the other. If we wish to find the pressure relationship of two sounds which are 37 decibels apart, we first regard the 37 decibels as being composed of 30 decibels plus an additional 7 decibels. Turning to our table, we see that 30 decibels represents a difference in sound pressure of 31.6. Seven decibels represents a pressure differential of 2.24. By multiplying the 31.6 times the 2.24, we see that the pressure differential represented by a difference of 37 decibels is 70.8. A sound which is 37 decibels greater than another has 70.8 times as much sound pressure as the other.

We can utilize the table also if we know a difference in power or pressure between two sounds and we wish to know what this means in decibels. Suppose, for example, that we know that one sound has 443 times as much power as another. We first break down this number, in terms of multiplication, into units which we can plug into our scale. Four hundred and forty-three times more power would mean the same thing as 100 times more power multiplied by 4.43 times more power. Turning to the scale, 100 times more power would mean 20 decibels, and 4.43 times more power would be about 6.5 decibels. When we add these two numbers together, we find that 443 times more power equals approximately 26.5 decibels. So one sound is 26.5 decibels greater than the other.

VI

INTENSITY IN SPEECH

As WE STUDY THE ROLE of intensity of speech in greater detail, we must turn our attention to some definitions of terms and concepts concerning speech intensity. The threshold of hearing (audibility or detectability) is the minimum effective sound pressure of a signal that is capable of evoking an auditory sensation in a specified number of trials (at each frequency) (51). Factors to be considered in determining threshold are as follows: (a) the manner in which the stimulus is presented to the listener; (b) the nature of the stimulus, and (c) The point at which the sound pressure is measured. The measurement of the response that is accepted is the level which will just excite the sensation of hearing at the particular frequency in question.

It is important to note that threshold and sensitivity are reciprocally related. That is, when sensitivity for a tone is very good, the threshold will be low. It will take less sound pressure to elicit a response of hearing for a frequency to which the ear is well tuned. On the other hand, at a frequency where sensitivity of the ear is not well tuned, it will take greater sound pressure to elicit a response of hearing. Therefore, if sensitivity for the tone is poor, the threshold will be relatively high. More energy will be needed to elicit a response of hearing. The measurement of threshold is performed by establishing a ratio between one person's threshold and the so-called normal threshold. Table VII lists those amounts of actual sound pressure, measured from a base of .0002 dynes per square centimeter, which are necessary to evoke a response of hearing from normal listeners. It should be noted that these amounts of sound pressure are those set forth in normative data established by the International Standards Organization in 1963. The norms are based upon responses of normal hearing persons between the ages of 18 and 25 who were

85

Speech Science

tested in sound treated environments in experimental situations. These factors are stressed because prior to this time another set of norms were in existence, entitled the American Standards Association norms of 1951. These earlier norms were based upon a public health study carried forth in many American cities during 1935 and 1936, in which various age groups and different testing environments were utilized. Using the 1963 International Standards Organization norms, a person must have better hearing acuity than was true with the earlier established norms in order to be considered a normal hearing individual.

TABLE VII

CALIBRATION DATA FOR AUDIOMETERS

Frequency (cps)	ISO-1964	ASA-1951	Difference
125	45.5 dB	54.5 dB	9 dB
250	24.5 dB	39.5 dB	15 dB
500	11 dB	25 dB	14 dB
1000	6.5 dB	16.5 dB	10 dB
1500	6.5 dB	16.5 dB	10 dB
2000	8.5 dB	17 dB	8.5 dB
3000	7.5 dB	16 dB	8.5 dB
4000	9 dB	15 dB	6 dB
6000	8 dB	17.5 dB	9.5 dB
8000	9.5 dB	21 dB	11.5 dB

Sensation level is the pressure level of a sound in decibels for a listener above his threshold of audibility; the sensation level of any sound reaching the ear is the number of decibels by which the pressure of a given sound exceeds the threshold of audibility for that particular frequency in question (52). Zero sensation level is the sensation level of hearing for normal hearing subjects. That is, a sound pressure of 6.5 decibels above .0002 dynes per square centimeter will elicit a response of hearing from a perfectly normal hearing subject at 1000 cycles per second. This amount of sound pressure, the normal threshold for 1000 cycles, is then termed the zero sensation level for 1000 cycles. On the usual instrument for measuring hearing, the audiometer, the 0 on the hearing loss dial at 1000 cps means a sound pressure of 6.5 decibels above .0002 dynes per square centimeter. If a person being tested can respond to 1000 cycles at 0 on the hearing loss dial, he is responding at zero sensation level. If another tone at 1000 cycles is presented to the same individual 20 decibels above this point, he is then being presented with a 1000 cycle tone presented at a 20 dB sensation level. Sensation level, then, refers to the decibel ratio between any given sound presented and the threshold of a particular individual for that particular sound.

The hearing area refers to all of the frequencies which the normal ear can detect, and all the range of intensities which that ear can detect. It expresses the relationship between sensations in our ear and the dimensions and magnitudes of the changes in the physical stimuli. The usual ear can detect frequencies between about 20 cycles per second and 20,000 cycles per second, will respond to intensity differences between the zero sensation level and a point of discomfort which is about 125 decibels above .0002 dynes per square centimeter at all frequencies. If we look merely at the intensity differentials involved in the hearing area, and limit our attention to only one frequency, the range of intensities between the minimum intensity needed to elicit a response and the maximum intensity which can be endured without too much discomfort is termed the dynamic range. As will be noted from Figure 22, the dynamic range is greatest in the frequency range from about 800 cycles per second up to about 4000 cycles per second. The amount of sound pressure needed to elicit a response in this frequency range varies from about 7 to 9 decibels above the zero reference point, and the threshold of discomfort is found around 120 to 125 decibels above the zero reference point. The dynamic range for these frequencies is then about 112 to 118 decibels.

Looking again at Figure 22, we note a bottom line indicating the threshold of hearing according to ISO norms. We note that this line divides audible tones from the inaudible, and also reveals that both low frequencies and very high frequencies must be made more intense to be detected. The top lines show thresholds of tolerance. After sound pressure elicits a feeling of discomfort, there is usually a reaction of a tickling sensation with slightly more sound pressure, and then finally a feeling of pain with sound pressure amounting to about 135 to 140 decibels above

Speech Science

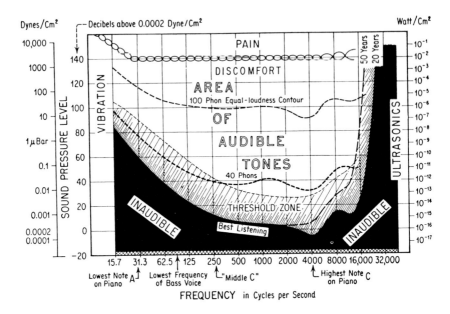

FIGURE 22. The auditory area for listening with both ears in an acoustic field, as in everyday listening, is bounded below by the threshold zone, by vibration on the low-frequency side, by ultrasonics on the high-frequency side and, practically, by the threshold of pain in the direction of high intensity. Below the threshold zone, tones are inaudible. None of the boundaries are sharp. Even under the best listening conditions, normal well-motivated young listeners may differ by 15 dB. The lower edge of the zone, labeled "best listening," represents the median sensitivity of a group of otologically normal young ears listening in a free acoustic field. The dips at 4000 and 12,000 are due to resonance effects in the ear canals, diffraction patterns around the head, etc. (The acoustic field is measured before the head is placed in it.) The high-frequency boundary becomes progressively lower with age. Two equal-loudness contours are shown for tones judged to sound as loud as 1000 cps tones at 40 dB and 100 dB SPL, respectively. Sound pressure levels (SPL) are given at the extreme left in dynes per square centimeter or microbars (μbar), next in decibels above the standard reference level, and at the right in watts per square centimeter. (Data from D.W. Robinson and R.S. Dadson, *Journal of the Acoustical Society of America*, 29:1284-1288, 1957.) (Reprinted with permission from Davis and Silverman, *Hearing and Deafness*, 1960, Holt, Rinehart and Winston, Inc.)

the zero reference point. This 15 to 20 decibel distance from the feeling of discomfort to the feeling of pain holds for most frequencies.

The difference between the zero sensation level, again referring to the average sound pressures needed to elicit responses of hearing from normal ears, and the thresholds of a given individual gives us information pertaining to the hearing level of the individual. This is the difference between this person's threshold level and the normal zero sensation level. If the hearing level becomes deficient enough, the person has a hearing loss.

We referred earlier to a loudness scale termed the Phon Scale. Loudness level is measured in phons, and is numerically equal to the sound pressure level in decibels, relative to .0002 dynes per square centimeter, of a 1000 cycle tone judged to be equal in loudness (53). Figure 20 shows loudness level contours compared with intensity levels. The curves are labeled with loudness level measured in phons. This scale is obtained in the following manner. A listener wears a set of head phones. He has at his fingertips a switch with two positions and a dial. With the switch in the first position, he hears a 1000 cycle tone at some fixed intensity, let us say perhaps 40 dB. When he throws the switch to the second position, he hears a different pure tone perhaps of 4000 cycles. By turning the dial, he is able to adjust the intensity of the 4000 cycle tone from the threshold of hearing to the threshold of discomfort. He is asked to turn the dial settings until the two sounds are equally loud. While doing so, he can flip the switch as often as he wishes to compare the loudness of the two signals. He decides on a dial setting which makes the loudness of the second signal equal to that of the 1000 cycle tone. The intensities of the two tones can be far from identical. Remember that the basic comparison upon which the Phon Scale was developed was the intensity level of a 1000 cycle tone presented at 40 decibels.

Any frequency sounding equally loud to 1000 cycles presented at 40 decibels has a loudness level of 40 phons. The loudness level of any given frequency is defined as the intensity in decibels of the 1000 cycle tone sounding equally loud to the given frequency. We will note from Figure 20 that a 100 cycle per second tone must be at an intensity of about 62 decibels to have a loudness of 40 phons, and an 8000 cycle per second tone of the same loudness will have an intensity of about 52 decibels. It will further be observed that the zero sensation level curve in Figure 22 now appears as a zero loudness level curve in phons. All frequencies which are barely audible appear to be at the same loudness level, and this loudness is barely discernible. It will further be observed that if one were to change equally the intensity level of different frequencies, which originally were of equal loudness, the resulting sounds are no longer equally loud. It will also be noted in Figure 21 that frequencies from about 800 to 1800 cycles share the same loudness level as that of 1000 cycles so that all frequencies within this range have the same loudness level as the decibel level of their intensity. The loudness of low frequency and very high frequency sounds increases more rapidly per decibel than does the loudness of tones of middle frequencies.

There is another type of scale of interest pertaining to the relationships between intensity and loudness. The Phon Scale of loudness level, which we have just discussed, is termed an "intensive" scale. This type of scale places measured sensations in order of increasing magnitude. A tone of 60 phons loudness is always louder than that of 40 phons loudness. But an intensive scale does not say how many times greater one quantity is than another; it tells only which is larger. There is also a psycho-physical scale known as a "numerical" scale. Such a scale makes it possible for an observer to declare: "Joe's voice is twice as loud as Al's, but Susie's lies halfway between the others." The numerical scale that has been developed to meet this use has as its unit of loudness the sone. Listeners judge a sound having a loudness of 2 sones to be twice as loud as a 1 sone sound which in turn is twice as loud as a 1/2 sone sound. Reference point for the sone scale is a 1000 cycle tone presented at a 40 dB intensity level. The loudness of this particular sound has been assigned arbitrarily a value of 1 sone. This type of scale seems to work well when considering the relationships of loudness of pure tones. However, variations in the power of the complex sounds of speech have rendered attempts to scale speech sounds on a sone scale somewhat fruitless. The scaling of the complex sounds have resulted in inconsistent and unreliable estimates. Consequently, differences in the power of speech sounds, which are complex stimuli, are generally reported in decibels. Figure 23 shows how the sensation of loudness in sones relates to the loudness level of a tone in phons. Notice that perceived loudness (in sones) is far from proportional to loudness level. By increasing the loudness of a sound from .1 sone to 10 sones, which would be an increase of 100 in perceived loudness, loudness level is increased from about 20 to about 66 phons. Referring again to Figure 20 we can convert the phon judgment, the difference from 20 to 66 phons, directly to intensity level in decibels. At 1000 cycles then, a hundredfold

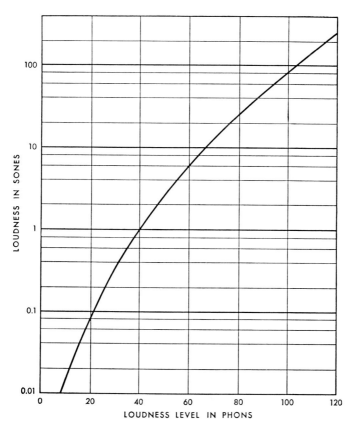

FIGURE 23. The loudness function, showing how perceived loudness (in sones) depends on the loudness level of the stimulus (in phons). (Reprinted with permission from Denes and Pinson, *The Speech Chain,* 1963, Bell Telephone Laboratories.)

difference in perceived loudness (in sones) necessitates a difference of 46 decibels, that is a change from 20 dB to 66 dB. Using the chart in Table VI, we see that 46 decibels, in terms of power, represents a power differential of about 40,000. So an intensity change of 40,000 has been comparable to a loudness increase of 100. Loudness does not change nearly as rapidly as intensity.

Thus far in this chapter we have been concerned with the way the ear perceives different intensities, and how these perceptions have been judged. Let us now turn our attention to some relationships of the power of speech. The first statement is that relative speech power can be measured by several methods. One such method is to measure the rate at which sound energy is being radiated at a given instant. This rate frequently rises to values higher than 100 times the average power. The average power is the total speech sound energy radiated while a person is speaking, divided by the time during which he speaks. The power of speech could also be described by the intensity of various syllables. The power of speech could also be described as the maximum value of one of the fundamental vowel or consonant sounds. When we analyze power of speech in this manner, we have some useful information by which to compare the relative amounts of power used to produce different phonemes. For example, vowels are usually much more powerful than consonants. The power of a syllable depends upon the maximum power of the vowel in the syllable. Fairbanks (54) has referred to this in the following paragraph:

> When we think about the intensity of speech, we usually have the peaks of stressed syllables in mind. This is a natural way of viewing the matter. If we wanted to describe the height of the Rocky Mountains, one way is to state the altitudes of the highest peaks. Within a syllable the greatest intensity almost always occurs during the vowel, so if we restrict ourselves to syllabic peaks, we are ignoring the consonants, as far as intensity is concerned. Just as the lesser peaks and foothills are important features of a mountain range, so consonants are important features of a speaker's intensity.

We have mentioned earlier that the intensity of normal conversational speech is somewhere around 65 dB. Let us now be more precise. The average level of a person's voice is 65 dB, when measured in a laboratory, with a microphone 3 feet from the speaker's lips. However, speakers are not always talking in laboratory situations, and listeners are not always exactly 3 feet from the speaker's lips. Recalling the inverse square law, we see that the intensity of the signal is going to drop off rapidly with distance. There is yet another ingredient which must be considered about the intensity level at which people talk, and that feature is the noise in the environment. If that same normal speaker has a listener 3 feet away from him, and is talking at the 65 dB intensity level, but is talking in a school cafeteria, the listener is going to have some difficulty understanding what is being said. This latter aspect leads us to a discussion of what is termed a signal-to-noise ratio. This is usually cited by the abbreviation S/N. A speaker talking at his 65 dB conversational level will be understood by listeners who are fairly close to him as long as the signal to noise ratio is at or better than + 30 dB. This means that the intensity of the speech signal is 30 dB stronger than the intensity of the noise serving as a background. As soon as the noise gets to be more intense than the signal, which would happen for example in a signal to noise ratio of —15 dB (the noise is now 15 dB more intense than the signal), the listener will have difficulty regardless of how close he comes to the speaker.

Perception of speech begins somewhere around 15 to 20 dB above the zero reference level. Almost total intelligibility is reached about 80 dB above the zero level. The rise in intelligibility associated with the rise in intensity takes place over about a 65 dB range. Below about 15 to 20 dB, there is essentially zero intelligibility. The listener simply cannot understand anything of what is being said, and above 80 dB, everything is understood, if the signal to noise ratio is appropriate. There is some evidence to show that signals can actually become too strong, and that as the strength of the signal approaches the pressure of discomfort, there may actually be a decrement in intelligibility. Figure 24 shows a report by Fletcher in which listeners perceived most syllables correctly as the speaker's intensity levels ranged somewhere between 50 and 75 decibels. As soon as the speaker was talking more loudly, the scores actually began to taper off. By the time the intensity of the signal reached 120 decibels the listeners were only identifying about 40 per cent of the syllables correctly whereas

Speech Science

at a 60 dB intensity level they were obtaining a score somewhere between 90 per cent and 100 per cent.

We have mentioned that the average power of conversational
speech is somewhere around 65 decibels. This average is obtained
from a range that probably extends from about 45 decibels when
a person is speaking softly up to about 85 dB when he is talking
either to overcome some noise which has come into the environment or simply trying to stress a point. When we whisper,
the average speech intensity probably drops another 10 to 20

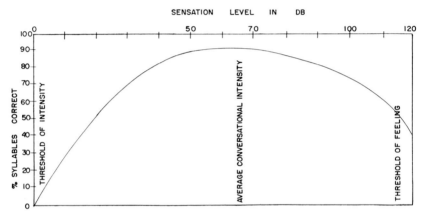

FIGURE 24. Relation of intensity level to recognition of syllables by judges.
(Reprinted with permission from Fletcher, *Speech and Hearing
in Communication,* 2nd ed., 1953, D. Van Nostrand Co., Inc.)

decibels. Table VIII reports the intensity levels in decibels of
various phenomena. It can be noted from this table that the
intensity level of a whisper is usually somewhere around 30 decibels, or about 15 decibels less than the person produces ordinarily
when he is speaking softly.

The oscillogram in Figure 25 shows the intensity at various
stages of production of the word "quite." The slow variations of
the wave rise slowly to about 1400 microwatts, the intensity of
the syllable, determined by the maximum value of the vowel [aɪ],
then decrease to 0 microwatts. Here we see that the intensity of
the syllable is determined by the intensity of the vowel.

The same information is conveyed in Figure 26, which is a
spectrographic tracing of the sentence "The rabbit ran across the

road." In a spectrographic tracing, frequency involved is indicated by the vertical aspect of the dark lines, intensity is characterized by the darkness of the lines, and time is shown on the horizontal dimension. Once again we note that the vowel carries the maximum power of the syllable.

Remembering that the power of weak speech (as soft as pos-

TABLE VIII

SPEECH IN DECIBELS AND CORRESPONDING FAMILIAR SOURCES

Speech and Hearing	dB	Source of Noise
Threshold of pain	140	Largest air-raid siren at 100 ft.
Feeling (tickle)	130	
Average threshold of discomfort (pure tone)	120	Airplane engine (close by)
Loud shout at one foot	110	
Discomfort felt for pure tones and speech	100	Boiler shop Subway express passing
Loud speech	80	Very loud radio
	70	Busy street Noisy restaurant
Average conversation	60	Average automobile Noisy office
	50	Quiet automobile Average office
Faint speech	40	Very quiet radio in home Quiet office
Whisper	30	Average dwelling
	20	Very quiet dwelling
Faint whisper	10	Outdoor minimum
Threshold of hearing	0	Reference level

(Reprinted by permission from Davis, *Hearing and Deafness,* 1947, Rinehart Books, Inc.)

sible yet not a whisper) has been shown to be about 40 decibels, we note that this power can be expressed as about .1 microwatt. The power of the whisper, which comes through at about 30 decibels, can be shown to be about .01 microwatt. A microwatt is the amount of power which, when released upon an area of 1 square centimeter, creates a pressure of .0002 dynes.

In a typical speech recognition test, a set of words is spoken and a listener or a group of listeners is asked to write down, repeat, or otherwise respond to the test items. One counts the number of words correctly recognized and this number, expressed as a percentage of the total number of words spoken, is taken as the measure of intelligibility. Tests of this type are called speech intelligibility tests, or speech perception tests, or articulation scores. The term articulation score is misleading because the articulation

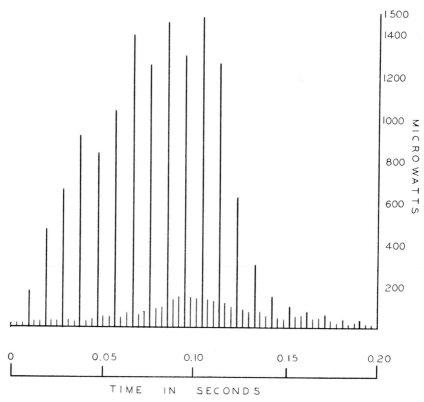

FIGURE 25. Oscillogram of the word "quite." (Reprinted with permission from Fletcher, *Speech and Hearing in Communication,* 2nd ed., 1953, D. Van Nostrand Co., Inc.)

test is actually a test of speech recognition, and not of speech articulation. The term articulation stems from the early research with this type of test carried on by the Bell Telephone Laboratories, in which the immediate concern was to see how intelligible certain kinds of telephone lines mght be under certain kinds of conditions. The term articulation was used in a sense representing how well the telephone line was speaking the words to the listener. The name adhered, and is still often used.

There are several types of speech which might be used in a speech intelligibility test. Fletcher (55) long ago discussed a sentence-intelligibility score in which sentences were used as the stimuli, and the percentage of sentences identified correctly yielded the score. He also discussed a vowel articulation score and a consonant articulation score, as well as a syllable articulation score. Each of these scores would be based upon the percentage of correct identifications of the particular variety of stimuli utilized. The two types of material most commonly used in the United States

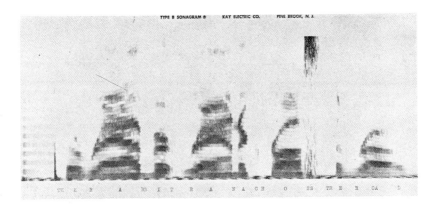

FIGURE 26. Spectrogram of the sentence "The rabbit ran across the road." The darkness of the bars indicates intensity. Note that the formant areas (*dark*) change during production of a diphthong. Frequency is located along the ordinate.

at this time are two types of lists originally prepared by the Psycho-Acoustics Laboratory of Harvard University, later modified at the laboratories of Central Institute for the Deaf in St. Louis. These are now described as CID Test W-1 and W-2, consisting of spondee word materials, and the CID W-22 list, composed of one syllable words. The spondee word lists are composed of two syllable words, such as "baseball," "whitewash," and "eardrum." Each of the two syllables receives some stress, although they need not receive equal stress. The other word lists, CID W-22, are composed of single syllable words selected in such manner that the speech sounds in the list occur with the same relative frequency as they do in spoken English. These are the so-called phonetically balanced or PB lists. Fletcher showed that word intelligibility scores will be poorer than sentence scores because a sentence can be fully recognized and understood even if every word in it is not correctly recognized. Fletcher reported that in a situation where a person can identify only 50 per cent of words correctly, he can recognize and identify 80 per cent of sentences correctly.

The frequencies responsible for intelligibility depend to some degree upon the particular type of speech material used. This fact has been demonstrated by the Twenty Band Method, where filtering devices are used to find 20 frequency bands, each of which contributes 5 per cent to the total intelligibility of the stimulus. These filters operate by cancelling out unwanted frequencies. Table IX shows the frequencies which have been obtained for each of the 20 equally intelligible bands of three different types of material, as reported by two different investigators (56). Notice that the low frequencies generally carry as much intelligibility as the high frequencies. This can be observed by noting the band width of frequencies included within each of the 5 per cent intelligibility bands. For example, under the report of the multiple choice words in the first column, the band width of the first of the bands extends from 150 to 230 cycles per second, a band width of 80 cycles. The next band width is 170 cycles, the next is 165 cycles, the next is 135 cycles, etc. The band widths remain about 200 cycles until Band 16 is reached, where the band width jumps to 400 cycles. Band 18 encompasses 900 cycles and Band 20, 1500 cycles. The same general statements can be made of the band widths included in each band of equal intelligibility for the write-down monosyllables. Band widths responsible for 5 per cent of the intelligibility of speech are largest at the high frequency end of the spectrum.

The overall spectrum produced when the effects of all speech sounds are combined can be studied. In this kind of analysis, a long sequence of connected speech is used, one long enough for every sound to occur many times. The energy level in each part of the spectrum is measured and summed up over the entire speech sequence. The summated energy for each part of the

TABLE IX

TWENTY FREQUENCY BANDS MAKING EQUAL CONTRIBUTIONS WHEN
EACH IS CONTRIBUTING OPTIMALLY

	Multiple-choice (Black)	Write-down Monosyllables (Black)	French and Steinberg
1	150- 230	300- 400	250- 375
2	230- 400	400- 500	375- 505
3	400- 565	500- 600	505- 645
4	565- 700	600- 690	645- 795
5	700- 850	690- 760	795- 955
6	850-1000	760- 850	955-1130
7	1000-1150	850- 950	1130-1315
8	1150-1350	950-1100	1315-1515
9	1350-1500	1100-1250	1515-1720
10	1500-1700	1250-1450	1720-1930
11	1700-1950	1450-1750	1930-2140
12	1950-2200	1750-1975	2140-2355
13	2200-2550	1975-2200	2355-2600
14	2550-2800	2200-2350	2600-2900
15	2800-3000	2350-2550	2900-3255
16	3000-3400	2550-2700	3255-3680
17	3400-3800	2700-2950	3680-4200
18	3800-4700	2950-3450	4200-4860
19	4700-5500	3450-5000	4860-5720
20	5500-7000	5000-7000	5720-7000

(From Black, p. 83.)

spectrum is plotted. The resulting curve is termed the long-time average speech spectrum and is shown as Figure 27. Notice that speech energy is generated by a speaker over the frequency range from about 50 cycles up to about 10,000 cycles. The energy is greatest in the 100 to 600 cycle region. This band width of frequencies includes both the fundamental frequency of the speech wave and the first formant. More regarding the term formant will be discussed later. Above about 600 cycles, the energy decreases steadily up to the high frequency end of the spectrum. At the high frequency end of the spectrum, at about 10,000 cycles, the energy is about 50 dB below the peak energy level which occurs around 300 cycles.

There are some general statements which can be made about the intensity of speech. One of these is that superior speakers generally show more variability in intensity than do poor speakers.

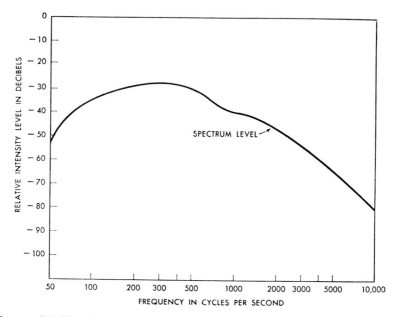

FIGURE 2.7. The long time average spectrum of speech. (Reprinted with permission from Denes and Pinson, *The Speech Chain*, 1963, Bell Telephone Laboratories.)

Good speakers have intensity ranges about twice the extent of poor speakers. Secondly, individuals tend to respond differently, in terms of intensity, to different voices. People generally state that female voices, at the same intensity level, sound louder than male voices. Persons ordinarily also talk louder when people are talking more loudly to them, and speak more softly when people are speaking softly to them. Black (57) reports that this phenomenon seems to be particularly true when speaking over the telephone.

There are also some general statements to make about the relative intensity of different parts of speech. Diphthongs and vowels are ordinarily recognized as the most intense phonemes which we utter, and voiceless consonants the least intense. Different studies show different results when investigating other factors of intensity, however. Tiffin and Steer (58) investigated the relative intensity of different parts of speech. They found that adverbs receive the greatest stress or greatest intensity, that nouns and adjectives receive approximately the same amount of intensity and fall behind the adverbs, that verbs and pronouns receive less intensity than the nouns and adjectives, and that finally, prepositions, conjunctions and articles receive very little intensity. Fairbanks (59) reports generally the same conclusions, stating that "words that carry the main burden of meaning, such as nouns and verbs, adjectives and adverbs, tend to have high intensity. Conjunctions, articles, prepositions and pronouns are usually spoken with very low intensity in comparison." The general conclusion seems to be that words that carry the meaning in our communication receive more intensity than do words or parts of speech which carry relatively little meaning.

Much information is available about the relative intensity of different classes or categories of phonemes. There are different methods by which the intensity of different phonemes may be explored. One of these is a measurement of intensity derived from monosyllables spoken disconnectedly without any stress or accent. When measured in this fashion, the intensity values of each sound are relatively independent from any kind of contextual influence. A second method of measuring the intensity of phonemes is to simply take a sample of conversational speech and then analyze the intensity values for each phonemic component of that sample of speech. Usually the intensity values obtained from this second type of measurement will be different from that of the first. Phonemes in the latter category will usually be either stressed or slighted, since the speaker will attach meaning to his communication and consequently stress certain phonemic elements. With this type of measurement, there is a definite contextual influence. The former method of measurement will reveal intensity values sometimes referred to as "normal values" whereas the latter type of measurement will yield intensity values sometimes referred to as "conversational values." Generally speaking, such research has tended to indicate that the normal values of different phonemes have a range of about 30 dB. There is a range of somewhere around 4 or 5 dB between the different vowels, and a range of somewhere around 25 dB between the strongest and weakest consonants. The weakest consonants have generally been reported to be the voiceless consonants. This means that the strongest vowel or diphthong we utter is generally somewhere around 1000 times more powerful than the weakest consonant which we utter. It is also interesting to note that certain vowels, notably the vowels [ʌ] and [ɪ] average considerably less power in conversational speech than in words spoken in isolation. Most of us tend to de-emphasize these vowels when we say words containing these particular phonemes in context. Fletcher (60) has reported that a vowel in an accented syllable ordinarily will have 3 or 4 times as much power as the same vowel in an unaccented syllable. Such a difference in power would produce a difference of about 2 dB. The vowels with greatest intensity are the so-called open vowels, those produced with the mouth open to greater extent. Such vowels would be [æ], [ɑ], [ɔ] and the diphthongs.

The consonants surrounding a vowel also seem to have an influence on the intensity of the vowel. House and Fairbanks (61) performed an interesting study in which they took the same vowel and surrounded it by different consonants, so that they emerged with nonsense syllables such as *ziz, sis, viv, gig, did, nin, mim,* etc. The intensity of the same vowel changed considerably when surrounded by these different consonantal environments. Certain consonants tend to make all the vowels stronger when surrounding them than do other consonants. For example, any vowel surrounded by the phoneme [z] had a greater intensity value than when that same vowel was surrounded by any other consonant. All the vowels had greater power when placed between voiced consonants or nasals than when placed between voiceless consonants. A vowel was more intense when surrounded by a nasal than when surrounded by a corresponding voiced homophenous phoneme. For example, the nasal phoneme [m] is homophenous with the voiced consonant [b] and with the voiceless consonant [p]. A vowel surrounded by [m] has more power than the same vowel surrounded by [b], which again has more power than the same vowel surrounded by the voiceless phoneme [p]. The range of differences in the power of a vowel surrounded by different consonants amounted to about 4 decibels. Figure 28 shows the intensity comparisons of the vowels surrounded by various phonemes. The entries show the average differences involved when the intensity values for all vowels were combined.

Hixon *et al.* (62) have reported that increases in consonant

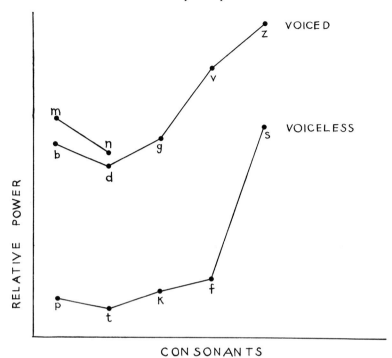

FIGURE 28. Consonantal influence on vowels. (Reprinted by permission from House and Fairbanks, "The Influence of Consonant Environment upon the Secondary Acoustical Characteristics of Vowels", *Journal of the Acoustical Society of America,* January, 1953.)

sound pressure levels, using the [ʃ] and [s] phonemes only, are accompanied by increases in intra-oral air pressure. Black (63) and Arkebauer *et al.* (64) have reported that intra-oral air pressure is greater for voiceless consonants than for voiced consonants. Measurements of intra-oral pressure are performed by inserting a catheter (usually polyethylene) into the mouth and along the upper teeth. An air pressure transducer is then connected to the catheter to sense air pressure fluctuations. Before the student protests too quickly concerning the artificiality of data obtained with plastic tubes in the mouth, he should understand that intra-oral air pressure is that generated by the air stream moving through the glottis, and is not identical to the pressure created, for example, by compression of the lips in forming a bilabial.

VII

WAVE COMPOSITION

THE READER MAY RECALL from the chapter on resonance, that a discussion of Fourier analysis was conducted. In this discussion, it was mentioned that any periodic wave, however complex, may be broken down into a number of simple sine waves having frequencies in ratios integral to the fundamental frequency and having also definite amplitude and phase relationships. Remember that the vibration of particles in a pure frequency is an example of simple harmonic motion, and that in simple harmonic motion, one producing a pure tone, the pressure changes continuously with the time elapsed. Its rate of change will be zero at two points: the maximum and minimum values (65). Simple harmonic motion has these properties: It is motion in a straight line; it is periodic to and fro vibration; at its two extremes of vibration there are moments of rest; its velocity is maximum as it passes through its undisplaced position, and its instantaneous acceleration is exactly proportional to its displacement.

When a particle has simple harmonic motion, its displacement is its distance from the middle point of its path, or natural position of equilibrium or rest, to positions on either side of the rest position usually regarded as positive when on one side and negative on the other. The positive concept means forward displacement and the negative concept actually means backward displacement.

Harmonic analysis is the breaking down of complex sounds into their component parts to discover what frequencies are present and what the relative intensities are of each component. This process is the method of isolating and measuring the amount of energy in the various partials or harmonics present.

When we turn our attention to the harmonic analysis of speech sounds, we must recall that the vibration produced by the vocal folds is applied to the vocal tract. The vocal tract is an air-filled tube leading from the vocal folds up through the oral and nasal cavities. Like all air-filled tubes, the vocal tract acts as a resonator. This means that the vocal tract will have certain natural frequencies of vibration, and that it will respond more readily to sound waves whose frequencies are the same as the resonant frequency of the vocal tract than it will to other frequencies. The fundamental frequency is the frequency of vibration of the vocal folds themselves. When the fundamental frequency is applied at one end of the vocal tract, that end being the glottis in the larynx, and is transmitted upward, the vocal tract will respond better to those components of the vocal fold tone that are at or near the natural resonating frequency of the vocal tract. These components will be emphasized and the spectrum of the sound emerging from the lips will peak at the natural frequencies of the vocal tract. This means of course that an analysis of a tone produced at the vocal fold level will be different from an analysis of the same sound as it emerges from the lips. These relationships are shown in Figures 29 and 30.

At the level of the vocal folds, several different frequencies will be generated. The one generated by the vibration of the entire mass of the vocal folds will be the fundamental frequency. In addition to this frequency being created by the vibration of the vocal folds, several other frequencies will also be present which will be produced by the segmental vibration of portions of the vocal folds. This means that even the vibration of the vocal folds results in a complex tone, and not a simple frequency.

The acoustic spectrum, which was mentioned in the last chapter, is defined as a graph showing the frequencies and relative intensities of the components in a complex sound. The acoustic spectrum, then, from a tone at the vocal fold level will contain several different frequencies. The most powerful frequency, however, will be that produced by the vibration of the total mass of the vocal folds. In a tone picked up by a microphone placed at the level of the vocal folds, such as a so-called throat mike used by bomber pilots during World War II, the fundamental frequency will be by far the most powerful component of the complex sound. The relative intensity of other frequencies produced at the level of the vocal folds differs to some degree with time. As soon as the vocal folds vibrate, the upper harmonics are strong. These harmonics dampen

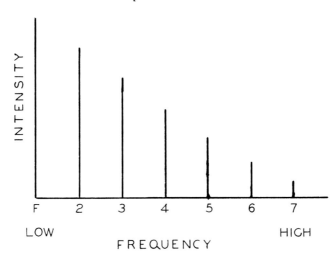

FIGURE 29. Analysis of vocal fold tone before reaching resonators.

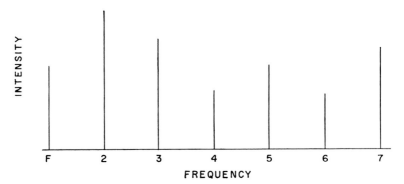

FIGURE 30. Analysis of tone from lips, after passing through resonance cavities.

out very quickly, however, and are termed "transients." The lower harmonics then assume prominence, usually within about 1/10 of a second after the tone begins at the vocal folds. These "harmonics" which have been discussed are components of the tone higher in frequency than, but integral multiples of, the fundamental. For example, a complex tone with a 100 cycle per second fundamental would have a second harmonic at 200 cycles per second, a third at 300 cycles per second and so on. An integral multiple is of course established by taking the fundamental frequency and multiplying it by a whole number such as 2, 3, 4, 5, etc.

Not all complex sounds are harmonic. Some are predominately harmonic with limited inharmonic energy present, and some are predominately inharmonic. Sound which is completely inharmonic is referred to as "noise." The frequencies in a noise vary randomly over time, and do not repeat themselves in a regular series. There are some special kind of noises which are prepared in certain fashions. For example, white noise is a sound in which all frequencies are present with equal intensity. Sawtooth noise is a sound in which frequencies are present in a special pattern, and are related in a particular fashion in respect to intensity, with the lower frequencies predominant. Figures 31 represents how a complex sound is derived from 5 separate components. The lowest component is the fundamental frequency, and the period of the wave will be that of the fundamental frequency. Any frequency in a complex sound which is not an integral multiple of the fundamental, and hence is not a harmonic of the fundamental, is referred to as a "partial." A partial then is any component of a complex wave. Sounds which are harmonics are also partials, but not all partials are harmonics. A synonym for harmonic is "overtone."

As one examines the wave form and spectrum of different speech sounds, he notes that most speech sounds fall between the two extremes of being periodic or aperiodic. Vowels are primary periodic, and achieve a steady state for a longer period of time than do consonants. On the other hand, fricatives and plosives are aperiodic transients. They go from one steady state to another, or from one vowel to another. Let us speak further regarding graphic representations of sounds. We have outlined, in Figure 31, the wave form of a complex sound. The wave form shows the amplitude and intensity relationships of a sound as functions of time. A sinusoidal wave form is simple and any complex wave form may be broken down by harmonic analysis into a sum of simple sinusoids. One cannot perform a harmonic analysis visually by looking at a wave form on an oscilloscope or a piece of graph paper, and therefore some other kind of graph is used to indicate the frequencies which are present in a complex wave and their relative amplitudes. The spectrum is a relationship between amplitude and frequency for a given time interval and represents

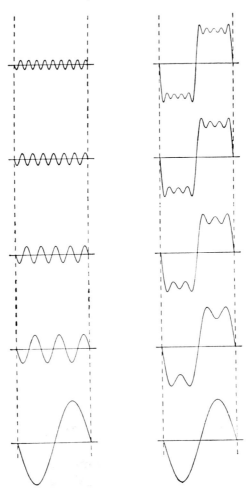

FIGURE 31. Simple waves add up to complex waves. The first five harmonics of a single cycle of a "square wave" are shown at the left. The series at the right shows progressive changes from a simple sine wave as each component is added. If enough additional odd harmonics were added, the composite wave would approach a perfectly square shape. (Reproduction by permission from Newman, E.B.; Boring, E.G.; Langfeld, H.S., and Weld, H.P. (Eds); *Foundations of Psychology,* 1948, John Wiley and Sons, Inc.)

the results of harmonic analysis. Samples of different wave forms and their associated spectra are shown in Figure 32. Note that the spectrum for a given frequency or pure tone is a single straight line whose height represents the amplitude or intensity and whose position along the abscissa represents the frequency.

If a complex tone is steady, and does not change in time, the spectrum obtained will be a line spectrum. A line spectrum is one in which the vertical lines are separate and represent discrete frequencies. As long as the complex tone is very short, however, and exists for less than one period, the spectrum becomes much more

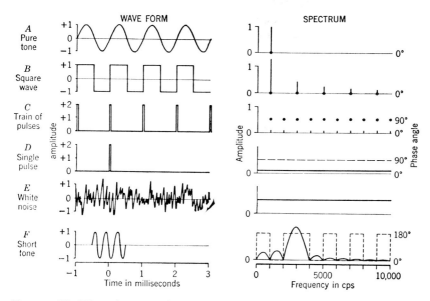

FIGURE 32. Wave forms and spectra. In each row, the wave form (*left*), showing amplitude as a function of time, gives the same information as the spectrum (*right*), which shows amplitude and phase angle as a function of frequency. (Reproduction by permission from Licklider, J. C.R., and Stevens, S.S. (Eds.): *Handbook of Experimental Psychology,* 1951, John Wiley and Sons, Inc.)

complex. The simple spectrum of a pure tone is obtained only after a relative long sample. The spectra of some sounds change very rapidly with time, and very different spectra are obtained from different time samples of the sound selected. Speech sounds are such rapidly changing sounds. An example of the wave form and spectrum of the vowel [a] is shown in Figure 33. The changes occur so rapidly that the analysis of the individual phonemes of

speech required the development of special equipment that could
portray continually changing spectra as a time function. The
instrument devised for this function is termed a spectrograph.
Examples of the output from a spectrograph were shown in Figure
26. Each portion of the spectrogram represents a spectrum of a
speech sound in a very small interval of time.

If a spectrum of a sound is constant over a long enough period
of time, the medium through which the sound is being propagated
is in a steady state during that time. Transitions in sound from one
steady state to another are termed transients. The pure tone is a
steady state phenomenon while it is on, but in the process of being
turned on and off a more complex spectrum is generated. These

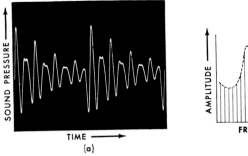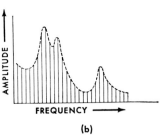

FIGURE 33. Wave shape and corresponding spectrum of a vowel sound:
(a) the wave shape; (b) the spectrum. (Reprinted with permission from Denes and Pinson, *The Speech Chain,* 1963, Bell
Telephone Laboratories.)

are described as the so-called on and off transients in a tone. A
short transient gives rise to a click which can be heard and detected. Speech is a long series of just such transient sounds. Remember that most of the vowels are periodic. They can be termed
steady state sounds for at least the short period of time while the
vowel is sustained. All fricatives and plosives, in addition to being
aperiodic, are also transients.

The introduction of the sound spectrograph for analysis of short
duration speech sounds gave rise to the term "formant." It was
mentioned earlier that as sound proceeds from the vocal folds up
through the vocal tract, the resonating chambers of the vocal
tract will selectively reinforce certain frequencies at the expense

of other frequencies. Recall that resonators do not create energy; rather they release the energy or permit it to be used more rapidly in the progression of the sound. As a result of the action of the vocal tract, a harmonic or a cluster of harmonics of relatively small importance in the original tone produced by the vocal folds may achieve dominance as the tone is acted upon by the vocal tract after it leaves the folds. These concentrations of energy become detectable on the spectrograph. The concentrations were originally called "centroids" and are now generally termed "formants." One of the more spectacular results of the study of formants has been the finding that certain formant areas (frequency areas having relatively high intensity compared to other frequencies in the sound produced) are relatively stable from one person to another for the same vowel. A given vowel will have its concentrations of energy at certain frequencies regardless of the speaker uttering the vowel, provided that all speakers involved are of the same sex. This means that a given vowel can be detected in a sample of vowels by identifying the frequencies at which the concentrations of energy occur.

Such an understanding of the meaning of the term formant and the relationships of formants between different speakers and different vowels gives rise to some concepts of quality. Quality is the attribute of tone by means of which tones that are alike in pitch, loudness and duration may be distinguished. We may differentiate between two different kinds of quality in the human voice, voice quality and speech sound quality. Speech sound quality involves a distinction between phonemes although they are similar in pitch, loudness, duration and voice quality. Speech sound quality is that kind of perceptive ability, based upon the locations of the formant areas, that allows us to differentiate between different vowels uttered by the same speaker. Recall, as was mentioned in the preceding paragraph, that these formant frequencies tend to be stable from one speaker to another, provided that speakers involved are of the same sex. There are differences in the location of the formant areas when considering the voices of men, women and children.

Voice quality, on the other hand, is that which enables one to differentiate between two speakers saying exactly the same vowel.

This distinction is produced between sounds which may be alike in pitch, loudness, duration and speech sound quality. Both types of quality seem to be dependent upon the action of the vocal folds plus the modifications imposed upon the vocal fold tones produced by the actions of the vocal tract. In addition to the size and shape of the air column in the vocal tract, the quality of the voice also seems to be dependent upon the texture of the pharyngeal walls. Tense, rigid walls tend to emphasize the higher frequencies resulting in higher sounding voices; lax walls permit the lower frequencies to be reinforced producing voices with a lower sound.

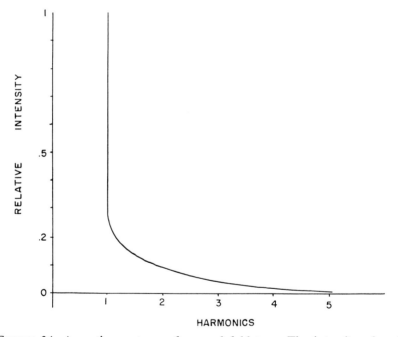

FIGURE 34. Acoustic spectrum of a vocal fold tone. The intensity of each harmonic may be determined in this manner:

Harmonic	Cubed	1/Cube	Intensity, assuming 50 dB for Harmonic 1
1	1	1.000	50 dB
2	8	.125	41 dB
3	27	.037	36 dB
4	64	.016	32 dB
5	125	.008	29 dB

It was mentioned earlier that the sound produced at the vocal fold level, if picked up through a throat microphone and then analyzed, will be different from the sound produced when picked up from the lips. Fletcher (66) has estimated that the intensity of any component in the vocal fold tone is inversely proportional to the cube of the harmonic number. In Figure 34 the frequencies involved in a tone picked up at the vocal fold level, and the intensity relationships of each of the harmonics are shown. If one assumes that the intensity of the first harmonic produced by the vocal folds in this particular case is 50 dB, then the estimated decibel intensity levels of the harmonics will be as shown in the figure.

Stevens and House (67) have discussed the spectrum shape of a speaker using a 125 cps fundamental frequency (a typical male voice). This spectrum is shown as Figure 35. Note the general agreement with the early work of Fletcher, and the predominance of energy at the lower harmonics. The magnitude of high frequency components decreases at a rate of about 12 dB per octave, slightly more than would be predicted from the early work by Fletcher.

Culver (68) has pointed out from the experimentation of Burroughs that phase relationships seem to have something to do with the interpretation of speech sound quality, but the experimentation has not revealed the precise details. We can say that phase certainly seems to give some information as to how a tone sounds to us. In Figure 36, the wave forms are shown of two complex sound waves. Each of these two waves is made up of 32 component sine waves of different frequencies. The wave forms of the two sounds differ because in the two sounds the crests of the component sine waves have different relative phase. That is, they arrive at different times relative to one another. While the relative phases of the components are different in the two waves, the frequencies and intensities of the components are exactly identical. Do these two wave forms sound alike? In fact, these two sound waves seem very different. The upper wave sounds somewhat harsh and low pitched, and also seems to be louder than the lower wave.

The ear is often said to be insensitive to phase relationships. It

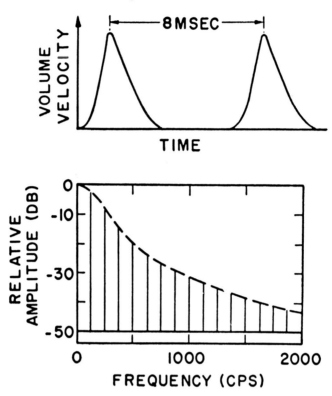

FIGURE 35. A typical wave form of the volume velocity of the glottal output for a fundamental frequency of 125 cps, and a Fourier spectrum corresponding to this type of wave form. The dashed curve describes the envelope of the line spectrum. The slope of the spectrum envelope at low frequencies is derived from Fourier analysis of quasi-triangular wave forms. (Reprinted with permission from Stevens and House, "An Acoustical Theory of Vowel Production and Some of its Implications," *Journal of Speech and Hearing Research, 4*:4, December, 1961.)

certainly is less sensitive to phase relationships than are some kinds of electrical measuring instruments. Apparently, sufficiently great changes or differences in phase can and do alter the quality of a sound, and the exact relationships between this phenomenon and speech sound quality or voice quality have yet to be completely understood.

One further note of interest is that the frequencies of the

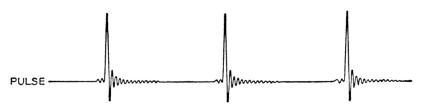

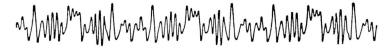

FIGURE 36. Two complex waves with identical frequencies and intensities, but with differing phase relationships. (Reprinted with permission from Van Bergeijk, Pierce and David, *Waves and the Ear,* 1960, Anchor Books, Doubleday and Company, Inc.)

formants produced by the action of the vocal tract may not be the same as those of the harmonics produced by the action of the vocal folds, although they may coincide. The formant frequencies are determined by the vocal tract, and the harmonics by the vocal folds. Vocal tract and vocal folds can act independently of one another. If the vocal folds remain the same, but the shape of the vocal tract has changed, differences will be noted in the formant frequencies. If on the other hand, the vocal tract remains the same, but the length of the vocal folds is changed, then differences will be noted in the harmonics of the vocal fold tones. The vocal tract apparently does not determine the frequency of the harmonics, but simply emphasizes the amplitude or energy of those harmonics which are similar to the resonant frequencies of the vocal tract.

VIII

VOICE QUALITY

W E LOOKED IN THE LAST CHAPTER at a sample of recorded speech as it emerges from a spectograph. We discussed the fact that certain frequencies would be reinforced by the action of the vocal tract and were known as formant regions. The formant frequency values depend upon the shape of the vocal tract. There are several formant frequency values for each vowel. When the soft palate is raised, shutting off the nasal cavity, the vocal tract is a tube about 7 inches long from the glottis up to the lips. For such a tube, if there were a uniform cross-section area along the entire length, the principle resonant frequencies would be found at 500 cycles per second, 1500 cycles per second, 2500 cycles per second, 3500 cycles per second and 4500 cycles per second. This would give us five different formant areas. In general, however, the cross-sectional area of the vocal tract varies considerably from point to point along its length. As a result, the formant frequencies will not be as regularly spaced as would be true for a regular uniform tube. Some will be higher in frequency, and others lower than the values cited above. The lowest formant frequency value found is termed the first formant; the one with the next highest frequency value, the second formant, and so forth.

When the soft palate is lowered, thus coupling the nasal cavity with the oral cavity, a basically different vocal tract shape is formed. The vocal tract begins as a single tube from the glottis, but now separates into two branches, one emerging through the oral cavity, the other through the nasal cavity. We now have different formant frequencies because of the additional nasal branch, and we have also anti-resonances that suppress parts of the speech spectrum. The nasal cavities also absorb more sound energy, thus increasing the damping, reducing the amplitudes of the formant regions. The speech wave produced depends greatly on whether

116

and where the oral cavity is obstructed, as in other speech sounds (69). Much of what we know about the formants of speech sounds is obtained by examining the sounds produced when the vocal tract is a given shape, rather than by explaining how these formants came about. There are certain factors which do emerge as being responsible for formant production, however, when formants of vowels are studied. Figure 37 is a representation of

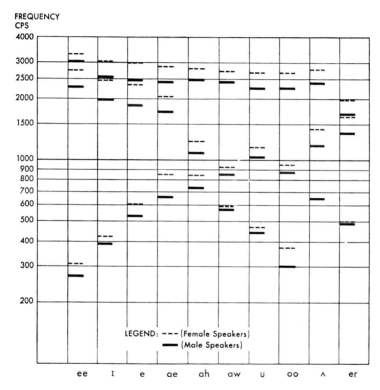

FIGURE 37. Average values of formant frequencies for ten English pure vowels. The vowels were spoken in isolated single syllable words. (Reprinted with permission from Denes and Pinson, *The Speech Chain,* 1963, Bell Telephone Laboratories.)

the average values of formant frequencies for ten different English vowels produced by a number of male and female speakers. Vowels were produced in one-syllable words, such as "heed" and "hid," with each syllable being spoken in isolation. Note that values are shown for only the first and second formant tracings. Table X is another interpretation of the same information given in the preceding figure. In Table X, the center frequency of each formant area is shown for the first three formants of each of the 10 vowels. The first two formant regions are probably of greatest interest to

TABLE X

CENTER FREQUENCIES OF FORMANT BANDS

	ee [*i*]	I [ɪ]	e [*e*]	æ [*æ*]	ah [*a*]	aw [ɔ]	u [ʊ]	oo [*u*]	v [ʌ]	er [ɝ]
				First Formant Frequency						
Male:	270	390	530	660	730	570	440	300	640	490
Female:	310	430	610	860	850	590	470	370	760	500
				Second Formant Frequency						
Male:	2290	1990	1840	1720	1090	840	1020	870	1190	1350
Female:	2790	2480	2330	2050	1220	920	1160	950	1400	1640
				Third Formant Frequency						
Male:	3010	2550	2480	2410	2440	2410	2240	2240	2390	1690
Female:	3310	3070	2990	2850	2810	2710	2610	2670	2780	1960

(From Denes and Pinson, *The Speech Chain*, p. 118.)

the speech scientist, because these first two formant areas change from one vowel to another. The upper formant areas are generally more constant for a given speaker, regardless of the particular vowel which he utters. These upper formant areas, then, are more directly connected or related to his individual vocal tract. Since the lower two formant regions change from one vowel to another, they are often termed "phonemic" since they are directly related to the individual phoneme.

Since the formant values for the lower two formants change from one vowel to another, it is interesting to see if one can determine any particular aspect of vocal production which might result in a change of formant area. For example, if one looks at the first formant values for each vowel, he notes that for vowels [i] and [u] the first formants are roughly the same. This same relationship is true for [ɪ] and [ʊ], the vowels [ɛ] and [ɔ], and the vowels [æ] and [ʌ]. This would tend to make one think that there is some relationship between each member of these pairs of vowels. The first member of each pair is a vowel generally classified as a front vowel, and the second member of each pair of vowels is generally called a back vowel. We are probably all familiar with a diagram known as a vowel triangle, shown in Figure 38. In the vowel triangle, the height of the entry of a given vowel represents the height of the tongue in the mouth in producing that vowel. Thus

FIGURE 38. Traditional vowel diagram, showing placement of tongue in oral cavity to produce a given vowel.

the tongue is highest in the front of the mouth for the vowel [*i*] and is highest in the back of the mouth for the vowel [*u*]. By looking at the vowel diagram, then remembering that formants are almost identical for each given pair of vowels lying horizontally across the diagram, one can conclude that the frequency of the first formant must have something to do with the height of the tongue in the mouth. The first formant region then, for a given vowel, is determined by the position of the tongue in the supero-inferior plane in the oral cavity. When we look now at values of the second formant frequency for different vowels, we note that the frequency values are highest for the front vowels and gradually diminish as the back vowels are encountered. One could conclude then that the frequency values for the second formant region must have something to do with where the tongue is located from the front to the back of the oral cavity, or is related to anteroposterior plane of the oral cavity. The frequency region for the first formant area is lowest when the tongue approaches the palate, and is highest when the tongue is furthest away from the palate; the frequency area for the second formant region is highest when the tongue is forward in the oral cavity and becomes lower in frequency as the tongue approaches the rear portion of the oral cavity. Figure 39 shows the relationships which obtain when the

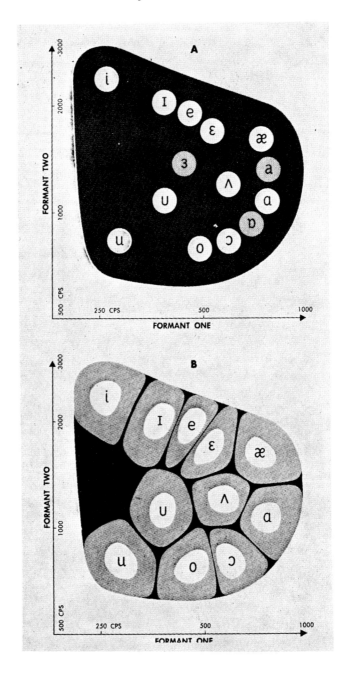

frequency values of formant one are plotted against the frequency values of formant two (70). In this particular rendition of this type of graph, the small center circles represent the center-most frequencies for the different vowels, whereas the larger irregular-shaped areas represent the general zone of each given vowel in General American speech. One will note that three vowels are not shown in this figure, the vowels [ə], [ɚ], [ɝ]. The first is the unstressed form of the vowel [ʌ]. The other two, the stressed and unstressed [r] vowels, are distinguishable only by the frequency of formant three, which is not shown in the figure. For these particular vowels, formant three is lower than for any other vowel. Their formant values for formants one and two coincide almost exactly with the location of the vowel [ʊ].

Studies dealing with the formant regions of different vowels have been carried forth for quite some time, with early work by Fletcher (71), Lasse (72), Lewis (73), Fairbanks (74) and Potter and Peterson (75). All of these studies generally show the same formant frequencies for the same vowel. There are some slight variations from study to study, but the general relationships seem to hold true for all studies. Remember that these given formant values for each different vowel will show up on a spectrogram as a dark area for that tracing of that particular phoneme.

The phonemes of American speech include vowels, consonants and diphthongs. A vowel is a voiced speech sound in which the vocal fold tone is selectively modified as it passes through the resonance cavities of the throat and head. There is relatively little obstruction of the breath stream. The different vowels are produced by changing the position of the tongue in the oral cavity. The vowels are built up temporally. That is, it takes some time to produce a sound. The production of a sound can be divided into three phases. The first we can call the build-up region or the

FIGURE 39. Acoustic vowel area. A: center of English vowels. B: Zones of General American vowels. (Reprinted with permission from Fairbanks, *Voice and Articulation Drillbook,* 2nd ed., 1960, Harper and Brothers.)

period of starting. It is at this point that the vocal folds move into the phonative position producing the first puff of air. The second phase is the steady state or the middle period at which time the sound is actually being formed. The final period is the falling-off phase in which the vocal folds move from the position of the last puff to the breathing position. Recall that the average duration of an isolated vowel is about .1 to .2 of one second. Since speech is so transient, it takes some time to build up energy for the particular phonemes. It is difficult, therefore, to obtain exactly similar vowels, even from the same speaker. The vocal tract is changing rapidly during speech.

Diphthongs are continuous glide sounds in which the articulatory mechanism is changing from one position for one vowel sound to another position for a different vowel sound. The initial position of the tongue, at which the glide begins, is usually called the "basic vowel." The basic vowel in a diphthong terminates in a smooth modulation of formants, or "off-glide," and the change is accompanied by progressive reduction of intensity (76). The off-glides are represented by vowel symbols, but are actually continuous changes of formant combination. Ordinarily these are rapid changes. It is the transition in the articulatory mechanism that actually gives rise to the diphthong. The tongue ordinarily proceeds from the basic vowel in an upward movement to the off-glide, and the mouth opening is usually smaller in the off-glide than in the basic vowel. The basic vowel is invariably stressed. It is longer in duration and intensity than the off-glide.

Consonants are produced by having some noise element present in the spectrum of the sound because of some degree of obstruction imposed upon the air emerging through the glottis. The consonants can be grouped by a number of classifications: One may speak of voiced and voiceless consonants, wherein the determinant is the action of the vocal folds; one may speak of stop, fricative, affricative and glide consonants, where the mode of determination has to do with the action of the articulatory mechanism, and one may speak of labial, dental, velar and nasal consonants, wherein the determinant becomes the place of articulation. More information concerning the different types of consonants may be obtained in any phonetics book. Here we shall state simply that voiced consonants are formed with the vocal folds vibrating, whereas voiceless consonants are formed without vibration of the vocal folds.

There is some general information available as to the frequencies which are of most importance for different classes of phonemes. Vowels are characterized by having most important frequencies lying in the area of the first two formant regions, which would mean frequencies roughly between about 200 cycles per second and about 2000 cycles per second. Diphthongs show frequency regions of greatest importance in the same general frequency area. Voiced consonants, particularly fricatives and plosives, show greatest frequency concentration between about 1500 and 4000 cycles per second, and voiceless fricatives and plosives, between about 2500 and 5000 cycles per second.

During the last fifteen years, much has been learned regarding the frequency areas of importance in consonants by studies performed with what are entitled "speech synthesizers." The speech synthesizer is an instrument designed to produce artificial speech, that is, speech which is produced by means of electronic circuitry. Electronic circuits are used to produce speechlike sounds with 1, 2, or any number of spectral peaks. The frequencies of these resonances can be set to any value within the range of audible frequencies. One of the main uses of such instrumentation has been to see how many such peaks, or formant areas, are necessary for satisfactory vowel recognition. Experiments with such synthesized speech sounds have shown that marginal recognition of vowels is possible by using the first two formant frequency areas. With the first three formant areas included, sounds are easily identified. Such experiments have also tended to show that the same formant frequencies may be indicated for the identification of different vowels. This has been observed in experiments where a listener was asked to identify vowels with known formant frequencies; the concept also agrees well with the scatter observed in Figure 40, showing the areas of frequencies of the first and second formants when different speakers produced the same vowel. Formant frequencies, then, do not always positively identify a vowel. Actually, no acoustic feature by itself ever completely identifies a speech sound. Speech recognition is based on the acoustic features of the wave, but is also affected by the expectations of the listener and

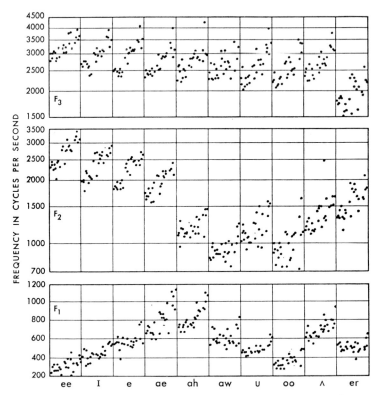

FIGURE 40. The formant frequencies of ten English pure vowels as pronounced by a number of different speakers. The notations F_1,
F_2 and F_3 refer to the first three formant frequencies. (Reprinted with permission from Denes and Pinson, *The Speech
Chain*, 1963, Bell Telephone Laboratories.)

by the knowledge of the speaker, the rules of grammar, and the
topic under discussion.

The Haskins Laboratories in New York were first to build an
instrument entitled the Pattern-Playback (77). This instrument is
roughly opposite in function to a spectrograph. We have discussed
the spectrograph, indicating that when a speech sample is applied
to the spectrograph, patterns are produced which are entitled
spectrograms, as were presented in Figure 26. The pattern-playback, on the other hand, takes a spectrogram-like pattern, scans it
with a light beam, and produces a corresponding sound wave.
Ordinarily the spectral patterns played back on this machine are

not spectrograms of persons talking. Instead, artificial speech is created by playing patterns painted by hand on a plastic belt. This artificial speech has a synthetic quality, a sort of "tinny" sound, but it can be recognized as being speech. The naturalness of the synthesized speech depends to some degree upon the amount of detail of the spectrum which is painted on the plastic belt. Usually, the first three formants of the vowels are painted on the belt for vowel identification. Figure 41 shows a spectrogram of the sentence "many are taught to breathe through the nose," and then the

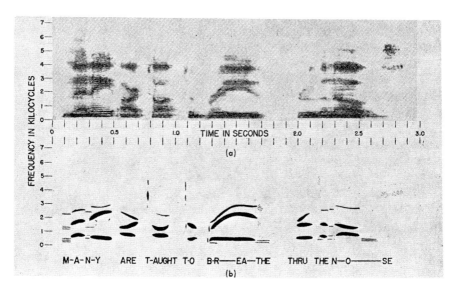

FIGURE 41. The (a) portion of the figure is the sound spectrogram of a naturally produced sentence; (b) is a painted pattern that can be played on the Pattern-Playback to synthesize the same sentence. Only the first three formants of natural speech are represented in the painted pattern. (Reprinted with permission from Denes and Pinson, *The Speech Chain,* 1963, Bell Telephone Laboratories.)

painted pattern of the same sentence which would be played on the pattern-playback.

The early experiments with pattern-playback consisted of vowel studies, in which spectral patterns were painted to include different formants, attempting to see how many formants were necessary for identification. As was already discussed, it was found that the presence of the first three formants was sufficient to identify English vowels.

In painting the patterns for the pattern-playback machine, it was found that a very short vertical mark was identified by listeners as a kind of plosive sound. The particular plosive which was identified by listeners who heard this "plosive burst" depended upon the frequency at which this burst was centered. Persons working at the Haskins Laboratories later found that the perception of the plosive depended to some degree upon the vowel which followed the plosive. The particular plosive consonant identified depended not only upon the frequency of the plosive burst, but also upon the formant regions of the following vowel. It was also discovered that listeners identified a plosive consonant, even when there was no plosive burst, if the frequency of the second formant was varied in the initial portion of the painted pattern. A pattern of this type is shown as Figure 42. The portion of the second formant where the frequency varies was called the second formant "transition." Patterns were then composed to test various degrees of upward and downward transitions. The test patterns were played on the pattern-playback and listeners were asked whether they heard the test syllables as *ta* , *ka* , *pa* , etc. Again, as was true with the plosive burst, it was found that the same kind of transition was heard as one plosive consonant or another de-

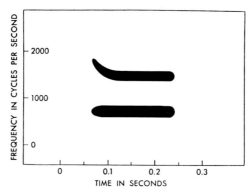

FIGURE 42. An example of second formant transition. (Reprinted with permission from Denes and Pinson, *The Speech Chain*, 1963, Bell Telephone Laboratories.)

pending upon the formants of the vowel which followed. Figure 43 shows all the frequencies of second formants and the degrees of the slope of the transitions leading into those formant frequencies, which when coupled with a first formant at 480 cycles, led listeners to identify the presence of the plosive [*t*]. In each individual case of this composite sketch, the second formants and the transi-

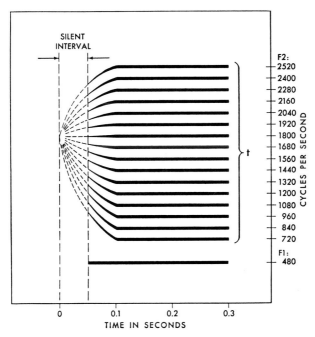

FIGURE 43. Second formant transitions perceived as the same plosive consonant, "t." (Reprinted with permission from Denes and Pinson, *The Speech Chain,* 1963, Bell Telephone Laboratories.)

tion leading into the formant were perceived as the consonant [*t*] followed by a vowel, where the first formant in all cases was 480 cycles. For the other plosives, the second formant transition tended to point toward different frequencies. The center point of identification of the phoneme [*t*], as shown above in Figure 43, is around 1600 cycles. For the plosive [*p*], the center frequency was around 700 cycles per second, and for the plosive [*k*], about 3000 cycles per second.

Results such as these are examples of the simultaneous cues

which are available in a speech sample from which listeners can make judgments about the presence of various phonemes. We have talked about both the plosive burst and the second formant transitions, each of which is helpful in the recognition of a different plosive consonant.

The evidence of such simultaneous cues also is useful in presenting to us the concept that a speech wave is a continuous event, rather than a sequence of discrete segments. We cannot say that a beginning segment (transition) of a vowel is related entirely with the recognition of either the preceding consonant or the remainder of the vowel following. It is concerned with the recognition of both. In the transition from the linguistics of the language to the acoustics of a speech sample, the sequence of discrete phonemes is transformed into a continuous flow of speech. The concept of the flow of speech reveals to us the importance of the study of the transitions from one phoneme to another. Often, the transitions are of as much importance as the actual particularized center frequencies of plosive consonants or formant regions of the vowels.

There is greater difficulty in trying to identify different fricative sounds. A fricative shows up on a spectrogram as a fuzzy segment produced by turbulence of the air stream. Experiments with synthetic speech indicate that the [s] and [ʃ] sounds are identified from other fricatives because the intensities of these two are greater than the intensity of the other fricatives. However, the fricative [s] is identified when most of the fricative energy is concentrated above 4000 cycles, and the fricative [ʃ] is identified when the energy is concentrated somewhere between 2000 and 3000 cycles per second.

The duration of the fricative segment on the spectrogram also is a variable. If there is a very short fricative segment, it is identified often as a plosive consonant. If one were to take a tape sample of the word "see" and then by cutting the tape reduce the length of the fricative segment by about tenfold, cutting the duration to about 1/100 of a second as opposed to the original 1/10 of a second duration of [s], listeners will often identify the segment as the word "tea."

Research continues with synthetic speech. One of the newer techniques is a speech synthesizer controlled by computer, and located at the Bell Telephone Laboratories. The computer is able to make the synthesizer produce speech which sounds much less "machine-like." Another facet of such research focuses on finding out how the tongue, lips and soft palate move during connected speech. The classical tool for such studies is an x-ray movie of the human head—a cumbersome and dangerous technique. More recently it has become possible to deduce articulatory positions from spectral analysis of the speech signal itself. One exploitation of this technique is a model of the vocal tract (proposed by Cecil Coker and Osamu Fujimura at Bell Telephone Laboratories) whose five parameters can be derived just from spectral measurement. With this setup it is possible to speak into a microphone and then, through the use of fairly complex analyzing equipment, produce at the output a cartoon version of the vocal tract in a motion picture or perhaps in a moving display on a cathode-ray tube (78).

We must also be aware of the fact that more than acoustic clues are involved in the recognition of different phonemes. We shall recall that in the case of the plosive consonants, we discussed the presence of multiple acoustic clues. We can eliminate one of these clues or cues, and the others remain, and still enable us to identify a particular phoneme. We must also keep in mind that the acoustic features are not the only cues available for speech recognition. Experiments with filtered speech have shown the importance of context in identifying different speech samples. Other studies have shown that the test vocabulary makes a large difference in terms of the ease of intelligibility of different materials. With test vocabularies of 2, 4, 8, 16, 32 and 256 English words, listeners who were taught and knew the test words were subjected to different kinds of filtering conditions. The scores obtained under the same conditions were much higher when the number of single test words was small. For example, under similar test conditions, when there were only 2 words from which to choose, the scores of the listeners averaged 87 per cent. When there were 256 words possible, again under the same test condition, the average score dropped to 14 percent. As we use the language of our experience, we learn to predict that certain words will occur after other words. These might be entitled linguistic cues toward the intelligibility of different speech samples. Persons originally thought that only acoustic cues made speech intelligible; it is now observed that acoustic cues are simply one type of information which might be available, and that the recognition of different types of speech samples might be much more complex than was originally perceived.

Let us now turn our attention to voice quality deviations. There have been several terms used over the years to explain different types of voice quality problems. Thurman (79) asked judges, composed chiefly of staffs of speech clinics and graduate students in speech in midwestern universities, to identify terms for voice quality problems which they thought were consistent. The terms identified by these judges were as follows: nasality, breathiness, thinness, stridency, harshness and hoarseness. Fairbanks (80) identifies only four types of voice quality problems: harshness, breathiness, hoarseness and nasality. Regardless of which particular view of the number of different kinds of voice quality problems is held, there is some information available as to the nature of the problem in at least some of these particular categorizations of voice quality deviations. Fairbanks speaks of nasality as being a problem, basically, of resonance. Nasality is imparted to the vocal spectrum by lowering the velum and coupling the nasal cavity into the vocal tract. When a vowel is adjacent to a nasal consonant, the consonant's nasality is often assimilated to the vowel as an extension of the normal transition. A vowel preceding a nasal consonant is more likely to be nasalized than one following, and certain vowels are more susceptible than others. Excessive nasality usually accompanies such organic conditions as velar insufficiency, velar paralysis, cleft palate or velum, or anterior nasal obstruction. The basic objection to nasality in English is that it is often unpleasant for listeners. Hixon (81) found in x-ray studies of nasal and non-nasal vowel production that there may be an incomplete closure of the nasal port for normal vowels. Adequate closure may not always mean complete closure, and several studies have shown that even in non-nasal vowels, there often is not complete closure of the nasal port. Kelly (82) found experimentally and Williamson (83) from clinical observation that nasality tended to be reduced if persons used a wider oral opening and greater articulatory movement.

Breathiness results when the vocal folds are too lax and fail to approximate completely as they vibrate, thus allowing a stream of air to pass audibly through the glottis and resonance cavities. Ordinarily in normal voice quality the vibrating vocal folds approximate in the mid-line once per cycle, closing the glottis and thus interrupting the air flow. In breathiness, there is insufficient firmness of the basic glottal closure. Breathiness is almost invariably accompanied by limited vocal intensity. The voiceless consonants of speakers with breathy voice quality are frequently more prominent than average (84). Breathiness sounds somewhat similar to whispered speech. The difference, of course, is that in whispered speech the vocal folds do not vibrate. In breathiness, on the other hand, the vocal folds are vibrating, but without sufficient closure. Some causes of breathiness are laryngeal pathology, such as a polyp (a small nodule formed on the edge of one or both vocal folds by extended use of the folds with insufficient rest) or some other type of node; improper coordination between the breath supply and vocal fold tension (there must be a proper relationship between infra-glottic air pressure and vocal fold tension for good voice quality); high chest breathing (clavicular breathing) with poor expiratory control as a result; allowing too much air to escape at the beginning of each sentence or phrase. Generally speaking, a loud voice will not be breathy. Loudness and breathiness are incompatible. Ptacek and Sander (85) have recently demonstrated experimentally that breathiness is less pronounced with increased intensity.

Harshness is characterized by irregular or aperiodic noise in the vocal fold spectrum. A common cause is excessive laryngeal tension. Such speakers often use an extremely low pitch, finding it difficult to maintain adequate intensity. The prominence of harshness varies among the vowels and in response to changes in the consonantal environment. Harshness may also be observed with voiced consonants. In addition to laryngeal tension, sometimes performed in an effort to produce a louder voice, harshness may be caused by poor coordination of the breath supply. Harshness may also be produced by an organic pathology in the larynx. Harshness may be heard on the ends of vocalizations where the voice makes a natural downward inflection. Sherman and Linke (86) found that harshness was heard on low vowels more than on high vowels, and more on tense vowels than on lax vowels. Rees (87) found that harshness seemed to be related more to fricatives than to plosives, with voiced fricatives seemingly related to harshness more than voiceless fricatives.

Hoarseness is familar to most of us as a symptom of acute laryngitis. It has been often cited that it is quite difficult to distinguish hoarseness from harshness (88), although this assertion is not supported by the data of Shipp and Huntington (89). Spectrograms from a hoarse speaker may yield characteristics which seem to be symptomatic of both harshness and breathiness. In addition to acute laryngitis, hoarseness may be produced by infections of the superior respiratory tract. It may also be caused by vocal strain, although functional causes are relatively rare since such laryngeal strain ordinarily will lead to an organic involvement if prolonged over a period of time. Hoarse quality and probably some qualities labeled harshness can be definitely produced by several types of organic problems in the larynx. Swelling, paralysis, or laryngeal growths or tumors of one kind or another can produce laryngeal malfunctions likely to produce both harshness and hoarseness.

Thinness is probably produced by tightly narrowed oral and pharyngeal resonance chambers (90). Usually a wider mouth opening will accomplish better resonance and avoid this problem. Thin voice may also be found in connection with too high a pitch level. Therapy is ordinarily directed toward lowering the pitch level and making greater use of articulatory movements.

Stridency seems to be related to excessive tension in the resonators (91). Since there is too much tension, therapy is directed toward relaxation. Stress is placed upon free relaxed production and an easy open tone.

In general the information we have on the acoustic evidences of voice quality problems is based upon subjective interpretation of spectrographic data. In a nasal voice, for example, there generally are fewer formants found than in a normal voice. One reason for such a finding is the fact that because of the coupling of the nasal cavity into the vocal tract, there is a shift in intensity of the first formant (92). Mysak (93) also reports extra resonance areas located between regular vowel formants. A spectrogram of a speaker with a harsh voice reveals aperiodic noise in all formant areas, chiefly observed at the beginning of a phrase. Breathiness is characterized on a spectrogram by aperiodicity throughout the entire vocal spectrum. Hoarseness, when observed on the spectrogram, is characterized by a great mass of noise obscuring all formants above formant one. The noise seems to begin about the level of the second formant and extends into the higher frequencies.

Let us keep in mind that it is the ear of the listener that actually determines the presence of a disorder or defect. There may be an undue distribution of energy in the partials, there may be a higher or lower fundamental than is present in most persons, there may be a great mass of noise throughout a considerable portion of the frequency area found in the voice spectrum, but if the ear detects nothing wrong, there presumably is no problem of voice quality present. Of course, some persons are undoubtedly more tuned to detect differences in voice quality than others, and what appears to be a problem to one person may go unnoticed by another.

In summary, voice quality problems are dependent upon the same factors which govern the quality of the voice. Those factors, generally speaking, are the original tone as initiated by the vocal folds and the modification of this tone by the action of the vocal tract. Many persons with voice quality disorders seem to be speaking below their natural pitch level. While this evidence points out a relationship between voice quality problems and low pitch, there is little evidence to show any relationship between voice quality problems and use of a high pitch level, except in the case of thinness. There is some question as to whether thinness should be regarded as a true voice quality disorder.

Although we have mentioned some general statements concerning therapy with voice quality deviations, the student must realize that each person demonstrating such a deviation must be treated individually. The general statements are set forth as possible guides for therapy, not as definitive planning for therapy in every case. Clinical work with voice quality problems is best planned in consultation with a physician who has examined the organic condition of the vocal mechanism.

REFERENCES

1. FAIRBANKS, GRANT: personal communication.
2. GRAY, G.W., and WISE, C.M.: *Bases of Speech.* New York, Harper, 1947, p. 83.
3. STEVENS, S.S., and DAVIS, H.: *Hearing: Its Psychology and Physiology.* New York, Wiley, 1938, p. 19.
4. CULVER, CHARLES A.: *Musical Acoustics.* New York, Blakiston, 1951, p. 30.
5. HIRSH, IRA J.: *The Measurement of Hearing.* New York, McGraw-Hill, 1952, pp. 10-11.
6. SWENSON, G.: *Principles of Modern Acoustics.* New York, Van Nostrand, 1953, pp. 101-102.
7. ANDERSON, VIRGIL A.: *Training the Speaking Voice.* New York, Oxford U. P., 1942, p. 110.
8. VON LEDEN, H., and MOORE, G.P.: Mechanics of the cricoarytenoid joint. *Asha, 3,* (No. 2): 59-61, 1961.
9. RUBIN, H.: The neurochronaxic theory of voice production—a refutation, *Arch Otolaryng, 71*:913-920, 1960.
10. FLETCHER, H.: Loudness, pitch, and timbre of musical tones. *J. Acoustical Soc Amer, 6*:59-69, 1934.
11. FAIRBANKS, G.: *Voice and Articulation Drillbook.* 2nd ed. New York, Harper, 1960, p. 123.
12. PRONOVOST, W.: An experimental study of methods for determining natural and habitual pitch. *Speech Monographs, 9*:123, 1942.
13. FAIRBANKS, G.: *op. cit.,* p. 122.
14. PRONOVOST, W.: *op. cit.,* p. 121.
15. FAIRBANKS, G.: An acoustical study of the pitch of infant hunger wails. *Child Develop, 13*:227-232, 1942.
16. CURRY, E.T.: The pitch characteristics of the adolescent male voice. *Speech Monographs, 7*:48-62, 1940.
17. *Ibid.*
18. MURRY, E., and TIFFIN, J.: An analysis of some basic aspects of effective speech, *Arch Speech. 1*:61-83, 1934.
19. SNIDECOR, J.C.: A comparative study of the pitch and duration characteristics of impromptu speaking and oral reading. *Speech Monographs, 10*:50-56, 1943.
20. FAIRBANKS, G.: Infant hunger wails, *op. cit.,* p. 230.
21. FAIRBANKS, G., et al.: An acoustical study of vocal pitch in seven and eight year old girls. *Child Develop, 20*:70-78, 1948; An acoustical study of vocal pitch in seven and eight year old boys. *Child Develop 20*:63-69, 1948.
22. SNIDECOR, J.C.: The pitch and duration characteristics of superior female speakers during oral reading. *J Speech Hearing Dis, 16*:45-46, 1951.

23. MURRAY, E., and TIFFIN, J.: *op. cit.*, pp. 61-83.
24. FAIRBANKS, G.: *Voice and Articulation Drillbook, op. cit.*, p. 132.
25. SNIDECOR, J.C.: Superior females. *op. cit.*, p. 50.
26. FAIRBANKS, G., and PRONOVOST, W.: An experimental study of the pitch characteristics of the voice during the expression of emotion. *Speech Monographs, 6*:104, 1939.
27. TIFFIN, J., and STEER, M.D.: An experimental analysis of emphasis. *Speech Monographs, 4*:69-74, 1937.
28. PHILHOUR, C.: An Experimental Study of the Relationships between Perception of Vocal Pitch in Connected Speech and Certain Measures of Vocal Frequency. Doctoral dissertation, State University of Iowa, 1948.
29. HANLEY, T.D., and THURMAN, W.L.: *Developing Vocal Skills.* New York, Holt, 1962, pp. 144-145.
30. TIFFIN, J.; SAETVEIT, J., and SNIDECOR, J.C.: An approach to the analysis of the vibration of the vocal folds. *Quart J Speech, 24*:1-11, 1938.
31. MURRAY, E., and TIFFIN, J.: *op. cit.*, p. 68.
32. WANG, W.S-Y.: Transition and releases as perceptual cues for final plosives. *J Speech Hearing Res, 2*:66-73, 1959.
33. PARMENTER, C.E., and TREVINO, S.N.: The length of the sounds of a middle-westerner. *Amer Speech, 10*:129-133, 1935.
34. MYSAK, E.D.: Vocal attributes of older males. *J Speech Hearing Res, 2*:46-54, 1959.
35. SNIDECOR, J.C.: Impromptu speaking and oral reading, *op. cit.*, pp. 50-56.
36. DENES, P., and PINSON, E.: *The Speech Chain.* Waverly, Bell Telephone Laboratories, 1963, pp. 136-137.
37. MURRAY and TIFFIN: *op. cit.*, pp. 68-69.
38. PARMENTER and TREVINO: *op. cit.*, pp. 130-131.
39. MYSAK, E.D.: *op. cit.*, pp. 46-54.
40. SNIDECOR, J.C.: Impromptu speaking and oral reading, *op. cit.*, pp. 53-56.
41. DARLEY, F. L.: A Normative Study of Oral Reading Rate, M.A. Thesis, State University of Iowa, 1940.
42. FRANKE, P.: A Preliminary Study Validating the Measurement of Oral Reading Rate in Words per Minute. M.A. Thesis, State University of Iowa, 1939.
43. KELLY, J.C., and STEER, M.D.: Revised concept of rate. *J Speech Hearing Dis, 14*:222-226, 1949.
44. STEVENS, S.S. (Ed.): *Handbook of Experimental Psychology,* New York, Wiley, 1951.
45. DRAEGERT, C.L.: Relationships between voice variables and speech intelligibility in high level noise. *Speech Monographs, 18*:212-218, 1951.

46. SNIDECOR, J.C.: Impromptu speaking and oral reading, *op. cit.*, pp. 97-104.
47. *Ibid.*
48. VAN BERGEIJK, W.; PIERCE, J., and DAVID, E.: *Waves and the Ear.* New York, Anchor Books, Doubleday, 1960, pp. 26-27.
49. MORSE, PHILIP: *Vibration and Sound*, 2nd ed. New York, McGraw-Hill, 1948, pp. 215-240.
50. VAN BERGEIJK, W.; PIERCE, J., and DAVID E.: *op. cit.*, pp. 29-30.
51. HIRSH, I.J.: *op. cit.*, p. 343.
52. *Ibid*, p. 338.
53. *Ibid*, p. 337.
54. FAIRBANKS, GRANT: *Voice and Articulation Drillbook. op. cit.*, p. 138.
55. FLETCHER, HARVEY: *Speech and Hearing.* New York, Van Nostrand, 1929, pp. 225-227.
56. BLACK, JOHN W.: Equally contributing frequency bands in intelligibility testing. *J Speech Hearing Res*, 2:81-84, 1959.
57. BLACK, J.: The quality of a spoken vowel. *Arch Speech*, 2:16, 1937.
58. TIFFIN, J., and STEER, M.D.: *op. cit.*, pp. 73-74.
59. FAIRBANKS, GRANT: *Voice and Articulation Drillbook, op. cit.*, p. 143.
60. FLETCHER, H.: *Speech and Hearing in Communication.* Princeton, Van Nostrand, 1953, ch. 4.
61. HOUSE, A., and FAIRBANKS, G.: The influence of consonant environment upon the secondary acoustical characteristics of vowels. *J Acoustical Soc Amer*, 25:105-113, 1953.
62. HIXON, T.J.; MINIFIE, F.D., and TAIT, C.A.: Correlates of turbulent noise production for speech. *J Speech Hearing Res*, 10:133-140, 1967.
63. BLACK, J.W.: The pressure component in the production of consonants. *J Speech Hearing Dis*, 15:207-210, 1950.
64. ARKEBAUER, H.J.; HIXON, T.J., and HARDY, J.C.: Peak intraoral air pressure during speech. *J Speech Hearing Res*, 10:196-208, 1967.
65. JUDSON, J.S., and WEAVER, A.T.: *Voice Science*, 2nd ed. New York, Appleton, 1965, pp. 278-314.
66. FLETCHER, H.: *Speech and Hearing in Communication. op. cit.* pp. 90-95.
67. STEVENS, K.N., and HOUSE, A.S.: An acoustical theory of vowel production and some of its implications. *J Speech Hearing Res*, 4:303:320, 1961.
68. CULVER, C.: *op. cit.*, p. 61.
69. DENES, P.B., and PINSON, E.N.: *op. cit.*, p. 64.
70. FAIRBANKS, G.: *Voice and Articulation Drillbook. op. cit.*, pp. 22-46.
71. FLETCHER, H.: *Speech and Hearing in Communication. op. cit.*, pp. 90-95.
72. LASSE, L.: Effect of pitch and intensity on the quality of vowels in speech. *Arch Speech*, 2:41-60, 1937.

73. LEWIS, D.: Vocal Resonance. *J Acoustical Soc Amer, 8*:91-99, 1936.
74. FAIRBANKS, G.: *Voice and Articulation Drillbook. op. cit.,* pp. 22-46.
75. POTTER, R.K., and PETERSON, G.E.: The representation of vowels and their movements. *J Acoustical Soc Amer, 20*:528-535, 1948.
76. FAIRBANKS, G.: *Voice and Articulation Drillbook, op. cit.,* pp. 47-56.
77. COOPER, F.S.; LIBERMAN, A.M., and BORST, J.M.: The inter-conversion of audible visible patterns as a basis for research in the perception of speech. *Proc Nat Acad Sci, 37*:318-325, 1951.
78. Speech—man's natural communication. *IEEE Spectrum,* 75-86, June, 1967.
79. HANLEY, T.D., and THURMAN, W.L.: *op. cit.,* pp. 165-167.
80. FAIRBANKS, G.: *Voice and Articulation Drillbook. op. cit.,* pp. 170-183.
81. HIXON, E.H.: An X-ray Study Comparing Oral and Pharyngeal Structures of Individuals with Nasal Voices and Individuals with Superior Voices. M.A. Thesis, State University of Iowa, 1949.
82. KELLY, J.C.: Studies in nasality. *Arch Speech, 1*:26-43, 1934.
83. WILLIAMSON, A.B.: Diagnosis and treatment of eighty-four cases of nasality. *Quart J Speech, 30*:471-479, 1944.
84. FAIRBANKS, G.: *Voice and Articulation Drillbook. op. cit.,* pp. 179-182.
85. PTACEK, P.H., and SANDER, E.K.: Breathiness and phonation length. *J Speech Hearing Dis, 28*:267-272, 1963.
86. SHERMAN, D., and LINKE, E.: The influence of certain vowel types on degree of harsh voice quality. *J Speech Hearing Dis, 17*:401-408, 1952.
87. REES, M.J.: Some variables affecting perceived harshness. *J Speech Hearing Res, 1*:155-168, 1958.
88. FAIRBANKS, G.: *Voice and Articulation Drillbook. op. cit.,* pp. 170-183.
89. SHIPP, T., and HUNTINGTON, D.A.: Some acoustic and perceptual factors in acute-laryngitis hoarseness. *J Speech Hearing Dis, 30*:350-359, 1965.
90. HANLEY, T.D., and THURMAN, W.L.: *op. cit.,* pp. 179-181.
91. *Ibid,* pp. 181-182.
92. DICKSON, D.R.: An acoustic study of nasality. *J Speech Hearing Res, 5*:103-111, 1962.
93. MYSAK, E.D.: Phonatory and respiratory problems. In *Speech Pathology,* edited by R.W. Rieber and R.S. Brubaker. Amsterdam, North-Holland Publishing Company, 1966, ch.8.

COMPLETE BIBLIOGRAPHY

1. ANDERSON, VIRGIL A.: *Training the Speaking Voice.* New York, Oxford U. P., 1942.
2. ARKEBAUER, H.J.; HIXON, T.J., and HARDY, J.C.: Peak intraoral air pressure during speech. *J Speech Hearing Res, 10*:196-208, 1967.
3. BLACK, JOHN W.: The pressure component in the production of consonants. *J Speech Hearing Dis, 15*:207-210, 1950.
4. BLACK, JOHN W.: Equally contributing frequency bands in intelligibility testing. *J Speech Hearing Res, 2*:81-84, 1959.
5. COOPER, F.S.; LIBERMAN, A.M., and BORST, J.M.: The inter-conversion of audible-visible patterns as a basic for research in the perception of speech. *Proc Nat Acad Sci, 37*:318-325, 1951.
6. CULVER, CHARLES A.: *Musical Acoustics,* 3rd ed. New York, Blakiston, 1951.
7. CURRY, E.T.: The pitch characteristics of the adolescent male voice. *Speech Monographs, 7*:48-62, 1940.
8. DARLEY, F.L.: A Normative Study of Oral Reading Rate. M.A. Thesis, State University of Iowa, 1940.
9. DAVIS, H., and SILVERMAN, S.R.: *Hearing and Deafness.* New York, Holt, 1960.
10. DENES, P., and PINSON, E.: *The Speech Chain.* Waverly, Bell Telephone Laboratories, 1963.
11. DICKSON, D.R.: An acoustic study of nasality. *J Speech Hearing Res, 5*:103-111, 1962.
12. DRAEGERT, C.L.: Relationships between voice variables and speech intelligibility in high level noise. *Speech Monographs, 18*:272-278, 1951.
13. FAIRBANKS, G.: An acoustical study of the pitch of infant hunger wails. *Child Develop, 13*:227-232, 1942.
14. FAIRBANKS, G., *et al.*: An acoustical study of vocal pitch in seven and eight year old girls. *Child Development, 20*:70-78, 1948.
15. FAIRBANKS, G., *et al.*: An acoustical study of vocal pitch in seven and eight year old boys. *Child Develop, 20*:63-69, 1948.
16. FAIRBANKS, G., and PRONOVOST, W.: An experimental study of the pitch characteristics of the voice during the expression of emotion. *Speech Monographs, 6*:87-104, 1939.
17. FAIRBANKS, G.; HOUSE, A.S., and STEVENS, E.L.: An experimental study of vowel intensities. *J Acoustical Soc Amer, 22*:457-459, 1950.
18. FAIRBANKS, GRANT: *Voice and Articulation Drillbook,* 2nd ed. New York, Harper, 1960.
19. FLETCHER, H.: Loudness, pitch, and timbre of musical tones. *J Acoustical Soc Amer, 6*:59-69, 1934.
20. FLETCHER, HARVEY: *Speech and Hearing,* New York, Van Nostrand, 1929.

21. FLETCHER, HARVEY: *Speech and Hearing in Communication,* Princeton, Van Nostrand, 1953.

22. FRANKE, P.: A Preliminary Study Validating the Measurement of Oral Reading Rate in Words Per Minute. M.A. Thesis, State University of Iowa, 1939.

23. GRAY, G. W., and WISE, C.M.: *Bases of Speech.* New York, Harper, 1947.

24. HANLEY, T.D., and THURMAN, W.L.: *Developing Vocal Skills.* New York, Holt, 1962.

25. HIRSH, IRA: *The Measurement of Hearing.* New York, McGraw-Hill, 1952.

26. HIXON, E.H.: An X-ray Study Comparing Oral and Pharyngeal Structures of Individuals with Nasal Voices and Individuals with Superior Voices. M.A. Thesis, State University of Iowa, 1949.

27. HIXON, T.J.; MINIFIE, F.D., and TAIT, C.A.: Correlates of turbulent noise production for speech. *J Speech Hearing Res, 10*:133-140, 1967.

28. HOUSE, A.S., and FAIRBANKS, G.: The influence of consonant environment upon the secondary acoustical characteristics of vowels. *J Acoustical Soc Amer, 25*:105-113, 1953.

29. JUDSON, J.S., and WEAVER, A.T.: *Voice Science,* 2nd ed. New York, Appleton, 1965.

30. KELLY, J.C., and STEER, M.D.: Revised concept of rate. *J Speech Hearing Dis, 14*:222-226, 1949.

31. KELLY, J.C.: Studies in nasality. *Arch Speech, 1*:26-43, 1934.

32. LASSE, L.: Effect of pitch and intensity on the quality of vowels in speech, *Arch Speech, 2*:41-60, 1937.

33. LEWIS, D.: Vocal resonance. *J Acoustical Soc Amer 8*:91-99, 1936.

34. MORSE, PHILIP: *Vibration and Sound,* 2nd ed. New York, McGraw-Hill, 1948.

35. MURRAY, E., and TIFFIN, J.: An analysis of some basic aspects of effective speech. *Arch Speech, 1*:61-83, 1934.

36. MYSAK, E.D.: Phonatory and respiratory problems. In *Speech Pathology,* edited by Rieber, R.W. and Brubaker, R.S. Amsterdam, North-Holland Publishing Company, 1966, Ch. 8.

37. MYSAK, E.D.: Vocal attributes of older males. *J Speech Hearing Res, 2*:46-54, 1959.

38. PARMENTER, C.E., and TREVINO, S.N.: The length of the sounds of a middle westerner. *American Speech, 10*:129-133, 1935.

39. PHILHOUR, C.: An Experimental Study of the Relationships between Perception of Vocal Pitch in Connected Speech and Certain Measures of Vocal Frequency. Doctoral dissertation, State University of Iowa, 1948.

40. POTTER, R.K., and PETERSON, G.E.: The representation of vowels and their movements. *J Acoustical Soc Amer, 20*:528-535, 1948.

41. PRONOVOST, W.: An experimental study of methods for determining natural and habitual pitch. *Speech Monographs, 9*:111-123, 1942.
42. PTACEK, P.H., and SANDER, E.K.: Breathiness and phonation length. *J Speech Hearing Dis, 28*:267-272, 1963.
43. REES, M.J.: Some variables affecting perceived harshness. *J Speech Hearing Res, 1*:155-168, 1958.
44. RUBIN, H.: The neurochronaxic theory of voice production—a refutation. *Arch Otolaryng, 71*:913-920, 1960.
45. SHERMAN, D., and LINKE, E.: The influence of certain vowel types on degree of harsh voice quality. *J Speech Hearing Dis, 17*:401-408, 1952.
46. SHIPP, T., and HUNTINGTON, D.A.: Some acoustic and perceptual factors in acute laryngitis hoarseness. *J Speech Hearing Dis, 30*:350-359, 1965.
47. SNIDECOR, J.C.: A comparative study of the pitch and duration characteristics of impromptu speaking and oral reading. *Speech Monographs, 10*:50-56, 1943.
48. SNIDECOR, J.C.: The pitch and duration characteristics of superior female speakers during oral reading. *J Speech Hearing Dis, 16*:44-52, 1951.
49. Speech—man's natural communication. *IEEE Spectrum,* 75-86, June, 1967.
50. STEVENS, K.N., and HOUSE, A.S.: An acoustical theory of vowel production and some of its implications. *J Speech Hearing Res, 4*:303-320, 1961.
51. STEVENS, S.S. (Ed): *Handbook of Experimental Psychology,* New York, Wiley, 1951.
52. STEVENS, S.S., and DAVIS H.: *Hearing: Its Psychology and Physiology.* New York, Wiley, 1938.
53. SWENSON, G.: *Principles of Modern Acoustics.* New York, Van Nostrand, 1953.
54. TIFFIN, J.; SAETVEIT, J., and SNIDECOR, J.C.: An approach to the analysis of the vibration of the vocal folds. *Quart J Speech, 24*:1-11, 1938.
55. TIFFIN, J., and STEER, M.D.: An experimental analysis of emphasis. *Speech Monographs, 4*:69-74, 1937.
56. VAN BERGEIJK, W.; PIERCE, J., and DAVID, E.: *Waves and The Ear.* New York, Anchor Books, Doubleday, 1960.
57. VON LEDEN, H., and MOORE, G.P.: Mechanics of the cricoarytenoid joint. *Asha, 3*:59-61, 1961.
58. WANG, W.S-Y.: Transition and releases as perceptual cues for final plosives, *J Speech Hearing Res, 2*:66-73, 1959.
59. WILLIAMSON, A.B.: Diagnosis and treatment of eighty-four cases of nasality. *Quart J Speech, 30*:471-479, 1944.

GLOSSARY

Absorption—The assimilation or taking in of sound waves which constitutes a lack or partial lack of reflection.

Acoustical Resonance—Any body of gas (air) which is free to vibrate has a natural vibrating period and is capable of acoustical resonance.

Acuity—Sharpness or acuteness, particularly of hearing.

Average Power—The total speech sound energy radiated while a person is speaking, divided by the time interval during which he speaks.

Bel—The unit of intensity (ratio); a logarithmic unit expressing the ratio of two amounts of power; named in honor of Alexander Graham Bell.

Breathy Quality—That quality which results when the vocal folds fail to approximate completely as they vibrate and air is audibly heard escaping through the glottis.

Central Pitch—A pitch which is used more frequently than the pitches above or below. Other pitches tend to group around this one.

Compression—A pushing together resulting in a more compact condition of particles in a sound wave.

Consonant—A speech sound characterized in enunciation by constriction in the breath channel.

Conversational Values—The value or power of a sound in normal conversation.

Coupling—Two or more resonators which are hooked together and respond as one body.

Crest—The upper half of a graphic representation of a sound wave; actually the maximum state of condensation (compression) in the wave.

Cul-de-sac-Resonance—A condition resulting when the nasal cavity opening is larger than the anterior opening of the nares (nostrils) damming up the tone in the cavity.

Cycle—One complete set of the recurrent values of a periodic quantity.

Damping—A vibrator will not vibrate for as long a period of time when in resonance because the energy is absorbed and radiated more rapidly from the vibrator. This is the damping effect.

Decibel—One tenth of a bel (usually written dB); a difference in power

141

of two sounds of 26 per cent; a difference in pressure of two sounds of 12 per cent.

Diphthong—A speech sound changing constantly from one vowel to another in the same syllable.

Duration—The length of time a given sound or silence lasts.

Dyne—A unit of force; the force required to move a mass of one gram with a velocity of one centimeter per second.

Dyne Per Square Centimeter—The unit of measurement of sound pressure.

Elasticity—That property of a body which causes it to resist deformation and thereby recover its original shape and size when the deforming forces are removed.

Forced Vibrations—Result when a vibrating body is placed next to another object and the second object is forced to vibrate with the same frequency as the first.

Formant—A frequency area having relatively high intensity compared to other frequencies in a sound.

Free Vibrations—The vibrations which exist after the driving force (generator) has ceased operation.

Frequency—The number of complete cycles in one second of time.

Fricative—Characterized by frictional rustling of the breath as it is emitted.

Functional—Affecting functions but not structures; opposed to organic.

Fundamental Frequency—The lowest partial in a complex sound wave. This is the tone produced by the vibration of the vocal folds before the air ever reaches any cavities.

Generator—A body being set into oscillation is moved by some force. This force is the generator.

Glide—A transitional phoneme produced while the speech structures are assuming, or moving from, a definite phonemic position. Such phonemes vary, both acoustically and physiologically, during their production.

Habitual Pitch—The central pitch used habitually most often by a particular speaker.

Harsh Quality—Characterized by noisy, rasping, unmusical tones. This quality is sometimes called guttural and sometimes strident, depending upon the pitch level's being low or high, respectively.

Hearing Area—The range of sounds which the ear can hear, encompassing low to high frequency and weak to strong intensity.

Hearing Loss—The amount of impairment of a person's hearing, measured in terms of a comparison between his hearing and that of a normative group.

Hoarse Quality—A mixture of harsh and breathy quality caused by irritation somewhere in the laryngeal tract.

Inertia—That property of matter by which it tends to stay in the same stage of activity. It tends to remain at rest if it is at rest, or tends to continue moving in the same direction if it is moving.

Inflection—Upward or downward pitch level change during phonation.

Instantaneous Power—The rate at which sound energy is being radiated at some given instant.

Intelligibility—The percentage of material identified correctly.

Intensity—Magnitude of force, energy, power, or pressure. Usually expressed in decibels.

Intonation—General direction of the pitch movement over a period of time. Includes inflections and pitch shifts.

Isochronous—A resonator is isochronous when it has the same natural vibrating period as the vibrator. Any impulse having this same period is also isochronous to the vibrator.

Logarithm—The exponent of that power to which a fixed number must be raised in order to produce a given number ($100 = 10^2$, $\log_{10} 100 = 2$; $1000 = 10^3$, $\log_{10} 1000 = 3$).

Logarithmic Scale—A scale where ratios between different values are expressed in logarithmic units.

Loudness—The psychological response to the intensity of a physical stimulus.

Loudness Level—Found by comparing this frequency and intensity to the sound pressure level of a 1000 cps tone which is deemed equally loud.

Mean Duration—The average duration of a given phoneme or pause, determined by averaging the duration of several attempts of each.

Mean Power—By which the slow variations of the speech power are shown without showing the fluctuations of instantaneous power.

Median Pitch Level—That level above which half of the audible frequencies fall and below which the remaining half fall.

Median 90% Pitch Level—The range omitting 5 per cent at each end in any one person. Often called functional speech range.

Mel—A unit of pitch so defined that a 1000 cycle tone 40 dB above threshold has a pitch of 1000 mels (a subjective unit).

Modal Pitch Level—The pitch found most often in a given voice.

Nasality—Utterance through the nose of non-nasal sounds.

Natural Pitch Level—That pitch best suited to the particular speaking mechanism of a particular person. At this level, speech is most efficiently produced.

Optimum Pitch—That pitch which psychologically seems to "fit" a person according to size, age, sex and degree of masculinity or femininity.

Organic—Affecting the structures of the organism.

Oscillate—To move in a backward and forward direction or motion.

Partial—Any component of a complex tone. The frequency does not have to be an integral multiple of the fundamental, as does an overtone.

Pathology—The condition of an organ produced by disease; a change of structure.

Pause—When there is no vibration of the vocal folds, or no air emerging from the glottis.

Peak Value or Power—The maximum or capacity intensity of a sound.

Period—The time required for one particle of a sound wave to go through its complete cycle; or the time required for a sound wave to travel one wave length.

Periodic—Occurring in a uniform amount of time. Each section being of equal time with any other section.

Phonetic Power—The intensity of various syllables.

Phase—The phase of a sound wave, at a given instant, is the part of the cycle in which the wave finds itself at that instant, relative to some arbitrary reference point. Usually measured in degrees of a circle.

Phonation—When the vocal folds are vibrating, as in the production of a vowel, diphthong, or voiced consonant.

Pitch—The psychological response to the physical stimulus of frequency.

Pitch Flexibility—Refers to the extent and frequency of occurrence of pitch changes and the rates with which these changes are made.

Pitch Level—A particular level (expressed in cps or tones above 16.35 cps) at which a voice is currently being produced.

Pitch Patterns—When a person adopts a particular habit of upward or downward inflections, upward or downward shifts, or staccato duration, and uses this pattern continuously.

Pitch Range—All frequencies capable of being produced by any given voice.

Pitch Shift—A change in pitch level occurring between phonations.

Plosive—A consonant speech sound characterized by blocking, then suddenly releasing, the air stream.

Propagation—To extend the action of; to carry forward through a medium.

Quality—That property of a tone which may distinguish it from another tone having the same pitch and loudness.

Rarefaction—A separating of particles in a sound wave resulting in a less compact condition.

Reflection—The throwing back or bouncing of sound waves off a surface.

Refraction—The bending of a sound wave from its straight line path due to temperature differences in the air.

Relative Speech Power—Can be measured in several quantities as average power, mean power, phonetic power, syllable power, or peak power.

Resonance—The seeming amplification of sound resulting from a reflection and concentration of sound waves in a manner that makes possible more output of the vibrating body, but with a damping factor.

Saw Tooth Wave—One in which the fundamental and all harmonics are present in random phase.

Sensation Level—The level above the threshold of a sound is the pressure level of the sound in dB above its threshold of audibility for an individual observer.

Sharp Resonance—The tuning is sharp if the response of the resonator is maximal.

Sine—The ratio of the length of this perpendicular (reckoned from the diameter of a circle) to that of the radius of a circle. The perpendicular is placed at right angles to the path of the circle as it is rotated. The shadow from a light source traces a certain type of wave which is called a sine wave. Any regular wave with only one component is termed a sine wave.

Standard Deviation—A statistical measure to show the consistency of scoring in a population (plus or minus one standard deviation from the mean includes 68% of all the attempts).

Syllable Articulation—Percentage of correct recognition of syllables presented.

Syllabic Power—The maximum value of one of the fundamental vowel or consonant sounds, usually depending on the peak value of the vowel in the syllable.

Sympathetic Vibration—A vibrator is held close to a resonator, but does not touch. When the vibrator is struck, the resonator also responds.

Voice Break—A sudden shift of pitch (usually one octave) which seems to occur near the period of adolescence in boys.

Voiced—Speech sound formed with vocal fold vibration.

Voiceless—Speech sound formed without vocal fold vibration.

Vowel—A speech sound uttered with voice and characterized by the resonance form of the vocal cavities; has five regions of power in addition to the fundamental.

Vowel Articulation —Percentage of correct recognition of vowels presented.

Watt—The unit of measurement of power; electrical power is the product of voltage times current; power is the rate at which energy is used.

Zero Frequency—16.35 cps on the Orchestral Scale. This is the frequency which is generally regarded as the lowest tone the normal human ear is capable of detecting.

INDEX

Abrams, M. H., 70
Absorption of sound, 141
Acoustical resonator, 42-45, 141
Acuity, 141
Adam's apple, 57
American Standards Association, 86
Amplitude, 14-16, 73
Anderson, Virgil A., 134, 138
Antinode, 27
Aperiodic vibration, 7
Arkebauer, H. J., 103, 136, 138
Articulation score, 96-98
Auditory sensitivity, 85
Average power, 141

Beat, 27-28
Bel, 78, 141
Bell, Alexander Graham, 78
Bell Telephone Laboratories, 68, 96, 129
Black, J., 99, 100, 103, 136, 138
Borst, J. M., 137, 138
Breathiness, 131-133, 141

Central Institute for the Deaf, 97
Central pitch, 141
Centroid, 111
Closed tube resonance, 43-45
Complex tones, 7, 46, 104-115
Condensation (compression), 16, 34, 73, 141
Consonants, 122-129, 141
Conversation values, 141
Cooper, F. S., 137, 138
Coupling, 45
Crest, 141
Cul-de-sac resonance, 141
Culver, C. A., 20, 23, 29, 40, 42, 44, 113, 134, 136, 138
Curry, E., 57-58, 134, 138
Cycle, 141

Damping factor, 7, 8-9, 45-46, 141
Darley, F. L., 70, 135, 138
David, E., 136, 140
Davis, H., 14, 77, 88, 95, 138

Decibel, 73-84, 141
Denes, P., 24, 27, 76, 91, 100, 117, 118, 124, 125, 126, 127, 135, 138
Dickson, D. R., 137, 138
Diphthong, 100, 122, 141
Displacement, 31
Draegert, C. L., 70, 135, 138
Duration in speech, 67-69, 141
Dynamic range, 87
Dyne, 74, 81, 142
    per square centimeter, 142

Elasticity, 6, 7, 142
Energy, 5
Equally Tempered Musical Scale, 13-14, 53-54
Erg, 73

Fairbanks, G., 60, 92, 101-103, 121, 130, 134, 135, 136, 137, 138
Fechner, G., 79-80
Fletcher, H., 51, 93-94, 96, 97, 98, 102, 113, 121, 134, 136, 138
Forced vibration, 142
Formant, 99, 110-111, 116-130, 142
Fourier analysis, 41, 104
Franke, P., 70, 135, 139
Free vibration, 39, 142
Frequency, 11-13, 142
Fricative, 128, 142
Functional, 142
Fundamental frequency, 41, 49, 107, 142

Generator, 46, 142
Glide, 142
Gray, G. W., 134, 139

Habitual pitch, 51, 142
Hanley, T. D., 50, 135, 137, 139
Hardy, J. C., 103, 136, 138
Harmonic, 105, 107
    analysis, 41, 104-105
    motion, 104
Harsh quality, 130-133, 142
Harvard Psycho-Acoustics Laboratory, 97

147